Detecting Accounting Fraud Before It's Too Late

Detecting Accounting Fraud Before It's Too Late

ORIOL AMAT

WILEY

Published by John Wiley & Sons, Inc., Hoboken, New Jersey.
Published simultaneously in Canada.
English version by Raffaele Manini, UPF.

For general information on our other products and services or for technical support, please contact our Customer Care Department within the United States at (800) 762-2974, outside the United States at (317) 572-3993, or fax (317) 572-4002.

Wiley publishes in a variety of print and electronic formats and by print-on-demand. Some material included with standard print versions of this book may not be included in e-books or in print-on-demand. If this book refers to media such as a CD or DVD that is not included in the version you purchased, you may download this material at http://booksupport.wiley.com. For more information about Wiley products, visit www.wiley.com.

Library of Congress Cataloging-in-Publication Data

Names: Amat, Oriol, author.
Title: Detecting accounting fraud before it's too late / Oriol Amat.
Description: Hoboken, New Jersey : John Wiley & Sons, Inc., [2019] | Includes
  bibliographical references and index. |
Identifiers: LCCN 2019003711 (print) | LCCN 2019005387 (ebook) | ISBN
  9781119566861 (Adobe PDF) | ISBN 9781119566878 (ePub) | ISBN 9781119566847
  (hardback)
Subjects: LCSH: Accounting fraud.
Classification: LCC HF5636 (ebook) | LCC HF5636 .A43 2019 (print) | DDC
  658.4/73—dc23
LC record available at https://lccn.loc.gov/2019003711

Cover Design: Wiley
Cover Image: © stevanovicigor/Getty Images

Printed in the United States of America

V10008600_030519

To Pilar, Mireia, Natàlia, Marc, Lluis, and Anna.

Contents

I consider myself an expert on corporate manipulation and fraud. I researched the issue extensively and was an expert witness in numerous lawsuits of corporate misinformation and fraud. I am also a CPA and have taught accounting for decades. So, I really didn't expect to learn a lot from yet another book about corporate fraud. What a surprise! *Detecting Accounting Fraud Before It's Too Late*, by Professor Oriol Amat, a well-known and prolific accounting scholar, is full of new facts, insights, and useful prescriptions about corporate fraud and information manipulation. What a delight to learn so many new and practical things from this book. It's also great fun to read. Did you know, for example, that fraud already existed in Mesopotamia in 1700 B.C.?

Information manipulation by public companies is prevalent. In the United States, more than 70% of public companies regularly beat analysts' consensus earnings estimates. This cannot be done without certain a "management" (an elegant term for manipulation) of analysts' estimates, reported earnings, or, in many cases, both. Accounting and finance research documents extensively numerous cases of corporate misinformation and reporting fraud. There is no doubt that this phenomenon is, regrettably, quite prevalent. But the evidence is scattered, and often anecdotal. There is, therefore, a need for a comprehensive, in-depth, and practical discussion of corporate fraud. This is provided by *Detecting Accounting Fraud Before It's Too Late*.

The book appropriately starts with a definition of financial reporting manipulation: intervention in the process of preparation of financial information to affect investors' perceptions. It goes on to note that 11% of all corporate-fraud cases involve accounting manipulations, closely behind theft and bribery. So, the book deals with a serious, worldwide phenomenon.

The main contribution of this book is in its wide scope. It opens with a fascinating historical perspective of infamous fraud cases: from Mesopotamia, through the Dutch East India Company in 1600, and ending with the recent scandals of Enron and Lehman Brothers. It then continues with a thorough treatment of information fraud, starting with the major means of fraud: accounting manipulations—using accounting procedures, such as manipulating the multiple estimates underlying financial reports, to change reported information, and real manipulations—cutting, or delaying expenditures, such as R&D, advertising, or maintenance to inflate reported earnings. The discussion of the means, or techniques, of fraud is demonstrated by multiple real-life fraud cases.

The book then moves to the important topic of who wins and who loses from financial information fraud. It turns out that in many cases the losers are the innocent bystanders: employees and customers who are seriously harmed by the implosion of fraudulent companies, like Enron and World-Com. So, this is an important societal issue.

Next is a discussion of fraud prevention and the role of corporate governance in mitigating fraud. Finally, and this is a unique and an important contribution of this book, the author offers an evidence-based list of fraud warning signs (red flags). For convenience, the individual warning signs are combined into a fraud index that yields a unique number. This is very useful: Investors can rank companies, using the fraud index, by susceptibility to financial information fraud.

Detecting Accounting Fraud Before It's Too Late is thus a very important contribution to the growing literature on financial manipulation and fraud. Investors, corporate managers, and public policymakers in economics and capital markets will find this book very useful. It can also serve as textbook for the many college corporate fraud and forensic accounting courses.

Baruch Lev
Philip Bardes Professor of Accounting and Finance
at New York University Stern School of Business

Introduction

Companies' financial information is essential for making decisions. For example, to study stock acquisition, grant a loan, or evaluate the company's management team. But there are many decisions regarding marketing, human resources, technology, or any other dimension of the company in which knowledge of the company's financial situation is decisive.

Therefore, it is essential that the accounts be reliable, because otherwise erroneous decisions can be made and in addition trust in the company may be lost.

However, problems of accounting reliability often occur. As an example, we recall a 2014 PriceWaterhouseCoopers (PwC) report that shows that in the two previous years, accounting fraud occurred in 11.2% of companies worldwide. It is 8.6% at the European level.

Accounting manipulation is a problem that causes concern, especially when it is repeated frequently, a circumstance that occurs mainly in years of economic crisis, since, with the fall of economic activity, the numbers deteriorate and more managers fall into the temptation to hide that things aren't going well. This concern motivates our interest in detecting fraud before it is too late.

On this topic, in 1996 we wrote the book *Creative Accounting* in cooperation with the late professor John Blake. Twenty years later the problem continues to exist, albeit with different dimensions, as the world of business, as well as the accounting and mercantile legislation, has undergone significant changes. In some aspects it has improved, but in many others it has gone backward.

This book describes and analyzes the nature of accounting manipulations, its motivations and also proposes several techniques to detect these practices.

In order to present the different topics in a more practical way, several real cases are described. Since some of these cases are recent events that are still being settled in court, the affected companies' names were omitted.

At the end there are suggestions that can help reduce accounting manipulations or, in case they occur, to detect them in time. The following figure shows the outline of the book:

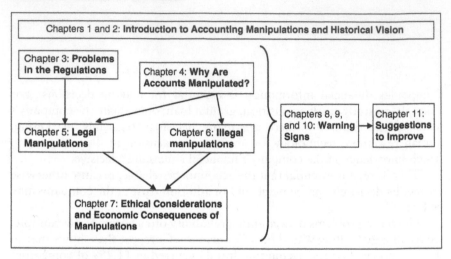

ACKNOWLEDGMENTS

Before beginning the presentation, some acknowledgments: First, to Raffaele Manini, who is responsible for the English version of the book; to Jordi Lapiedra Cros, Josep María López Serra, and Beatriz Calvo Vallejo, who have made contributions included in Appendices 1 and 2; to Andrei Boar and Clara Calabuig, who helped me in the analysis of the Olympus case. I also appreciate the suggestions received from Tomàs Casanovas; Daniel Faura, president of the Col.legi d'Auditors-Censors Jurats de Comptes de Catalunya; the Board Members at ACCID (Fernando Campa, Carlos Puig de Travi, Xavier Subirats, Gemma Soligó, Joaquim Rabaseda); as well as Nicola Eusebio, Manel Haro, and Marc Oliveras. Finally, I also appreciate the collaboration of Bianca Regina Held for her insights regarding the translation of the book.

CHAPTER 1

Fraud and Accounting Manipulations

A gray area where the accounting is being perverted; where managers are cutting corners; and where earnings reports reflect the desires of management rather than the underlying financial performance of the company.

—Arthur Levitt, Chairman of the SEC (Securities and Exchange Commission, US stock market regulator and supervisor), 1998

1.1 FRAUD AND ITS EFFECTS

A fraud is the action of deceiving someone to obtain an unjust or illegal benefit. According to the Association of Certified Fraud Examiners (ACFE— the international reference organization in relation to fraud detection), the main types of business frauds are:

- Theft of assets: cash, overpriced merchandise, inflated expenses, employees who are paid but aren't working.
- Corruption: conflict of interests, bribery, illegal gifts, extortion.
- Accounting manipulation: overvaluation (or undervaluation) of assets, liabilities, expenses, and income. (ACFE 2016)

In recent years, the relevance of cybercrime or computer crime, which is fraud done through information technology (IT) tools or with the aim to destroy and damage computers, electronic media, and internet networks, has been increasing. Thus, according to a PricewaterhouseCoopers (PwC) global survey regarding business fraud, cybercrimes are already the second most frequent type of crime behind assets theft (PwC 2016).

Continuing with the ACFE (2016), the different types of fraud cost companies around 5% of their sales figure. This is a very relevant loss if we compare it, for example, to the average profit of companies, which in good years is around 3% of sales (ACCID, 2016). This loss is caused by accounting manipulations (68%), asset theft (21%), and corruption (11%) of the total losses caused by business frauds.

In another study (KPMG, 2010) referring to Europe, 34.5% of executives surveyed indicated that their companies had been subject to some form of fraud in the past 12 months. Of all frauds, 11% were accounting manipulations, the third most important behind theft (28%) and bribery and corruption (13%). These data show that accounting manipulation is a very important issue due to its frequency and the losses it generates.

Accounting manipulation consists in intervening in the process of preparation of the financial information in order to ensure that the accounts present a different image than the one it would offer if the manipulation hadn't been done. It is a serious problem, because it affects the reliability of the accounts. Manipulations are done so the accounts reflect what executives and managers want them to. This way, the reality isn't reported and users of the accounts are deceived.

1.2 MODIFYING COMPANIES' FINANCIAL INFORMATION

Accounts can be modified through accounting notes or real transactions, which can be legal or illegal (see Figure 1.1):

- **Legal accounting manipulations:** These are postings that, in principle, do not infringe the accounting regulations, since they take advantage of the alternatives established in the legislation, the possibilities of making

	Accounting Manipulations	Actual Transactions
Legal	These are manipulations (see Chapter 5) that take advantage of: • The alternatives provided in the legislation • The possibilities of performing more or less optimistic forecasts • The legal gaps in aspects not regulated by the regulations	Perform actual transactions that affect companies' accounts (for example, advance or delay a transaction; or sell to clients with low credit rating).
Illegal	Accounting manipulations that violate the legislation (see Chapter 6). For example, conceal or inflate assets, debts, sales, or expenses.	Actual operations that aren't authorized by current legislation (for example, illegal transactions with companies located in tax havens).

FIGURE 1.1 Classification of account manipulation practices

more or less optimistic estimations and the legal gaps. Many authors call this type of manipulation *creative accounting*, although there isn't unanimity, as some people use this denomination to refer to illegal accounting manipulations. This topic is expanded on in Chapter 5.

- **Illegal accounting manipulations:** These are practices not allowed by current legislation (concealing sales or expenses, posting fictitious sales or expenses, concealing assets or debts, and so on). By violating the current legislation they can have legal consequences as they are accounting offenses. It is a topic that is expanded on in Chapter 6.
- **Legal real transactions:** These are real and legal operations designed to make the accounts show the image of interest. Examples of this are:
  - Selling properties to generate exceptional results in the desired moment.
  - Selling assets and then repurchasing them to materialize results.
  - Delaying the delivery of merchandise so it enters the next accounting year.
  - Advancing or delaying investments.
  - Increasing or reducing expenses easily modifiable by the company, such as training or advertising.
  - Invoicing between companies of a group to transfer results among themselves.
  - Increasing the sale of products to distributors (increasing excessively their warehouses) with the aim to improve results.
- **Illegal actual transactions:** These are actual operations that are not legal. Examples would be sales at prices different from market prices through third companies or subsidiaries in tax havens, which alter the company's profits, assets, or liabilities.

INFLATING THE BENEFITS OF COCA-COLA IN JAPAN WITH ACTUAL TRANSACTIONS

Between 1997 and 1999, Coca-Cola Japan modified the commercial conditions to its distributors so they would buy more, although it excessively increased their warehouse inventories. At the end of 1999, the distributors' warehouse levels had increased by 60% and were unsustainable. Coca-Cola told the SEC that it would modify its policy to reduce the distributors' warehouse, but the SEC described this whole operation as "misleading" and that it had been done to fictitiously inflate profits to meet the analysts' profit estimates.

1.3 CALLING THINGS BY THEIR NAME: FROM CREATIVE ACCOUNTING TO BIG BATHS

There are several names for accounting manipulations. Thus, in the United Kingdom, when referring to accounting manipulations the expression *creative accounting* is used. The term creative accounting is also used by many authors to refer to accounting manipulations done without violating current legislation. *Aggressive accounting* refers to manipulations done to increase profits.

The term *earnings management* is predominant in the United States and usually refers to legal accounting manipulations. On the other hand, when the manipulations are illegal, they are called *earnings manipulations*. Although these denominations seem to refer only to manipulations that affect earnings, in practice, they are used for all types of accounting manipulations.

In the United States, terms like *accounting shenanigans* and *income smoothing* are also used. Income smoothing aims to avoid the negative effects of the volatility of the results. It is a variant of earnings management that consists in transferring results from one year to another, reducing the earnings in good years and thus being able to increase them in following years. This transfer is done, for example, by recording significant deteriorations in one year, which are annulled in a future year. This way, the profit of the first year is reduced and, instead, it increases in the future.

Income smoothing can be done with three types of practices:

1. Year in which the transaction takes place. For example, a property can be sold at the end of December or, at the beginning of January and, therefore, in the following accounting year. By choosing the specific moment in which the transaction is done, we can determine the result of each year.
2. Allocation of expenses and income throughout different years. For example, depreciations and provisions are items that can be distributed over a greater or a lesser number of years.
3. Place where an item is classified. For example, an item of expenses or income can be included in ordinary or exceptional results (or results of continued or discontinued operations) according to the interest, thus varying the image offered by the accounts.

The two examples in Figure 1.2 show the difference in the earnings caused by the income smoothing practice.

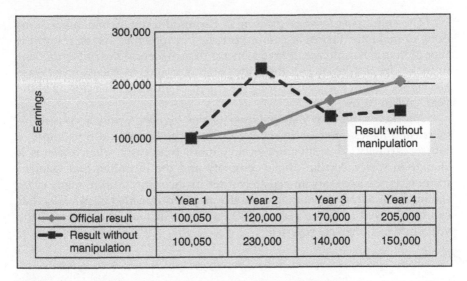

	Year 1	Year 2	Year 3	Year 4
Official result	100,050	120,000	170,000	205,000
Result without manipulation	100,050	230,000	140,000	150,000

FIGURE 1.2 A bank's result with and without income smoothing

Income Smoothing at Nortel

In 2007, Nortel Networks, an American company of telecommunications and IT, was accused by the Securities and Exchange Commission (SEC) of accounting fraud for fraudulently reducing (with an excess of provisions) the earnings of 2002 by 350 million dollars. This accounting fraud allowed transforming the losses of 2003 into profits by annulling the excess of provisions of the previous year.

Income Smoothing at a Bank

A real bank, in year 2, considerably raised the goodwill's impairment of several subsidiaries, with the aim of reducing that year's earnings that had been very high. This manipulation (see Figure 1.2), consisting of some extremely pessimistic estimates regarding the future of the subsidiaries, enabled increasing the profits of years 3 and 4. On the other hand, the declared earnings (see continuous line) increase every year, which presents a more favorable situation. Income smoothing gives those who do it an additional advantage that allows making use of privileged information. For example, if a company lowers its profits aiming to increase them in the future, it is information that allows anticipating that in the future, the price of the company's shares will increase (when the increase in profit is reported).

The expression *window dressing* is also used to refer to manipulations done to make the figures at end of year the best possible. Examples of this type of manipulations are, delay payments to providers at the end of the year to make the cash balance higher, offer high discounts to clients to increase December's sales, postpone posting the expenses until after the closing of the year, and so forth.

Another variant of manipulation is the *big bath*, which consists in increasing losses one year to reverse them in the future and thus improve future earnings. This situation occurs more frequently when there is a change in the leadership of the company and the incoming management formulates the accounts immediately after its incorporation. In many cases the big bath allows generating excessive provisions, called *cookie jar*, that can be reverted in future years and, as a result, increase the profits of the years in which they are reverted.

EXAMPLE OF PROJECTION OF LOSSES COINCIDING WITH THE CHANGE IN THE BOARD OF DIRECTORS

Figure 1.3 shows the example of the result of a real company where, in the years of renewal of the board of directors (2008 and 2014), significant negative results occurred in the first accounts formulated by the new board of directors.

	2007	2008 Year with change of board of directors	2009	2009	2010	2011	2012	2013	2014 Year with change of board of directors	2015	2016
Result	+16	−72	+9	+35	+23	+15	+31	+167	−65	+14	+49

FIGURE 1.3 Results of a company in millions of euros. The accounts of 2008 and 2014 were drawn up by the incoming board of directors

Another term associated to manipulation is *impression management*, which consists in presenting the accounts with data and graphs that highlight the positive aspects and hide the negative. This way, they are able to favorably impress shareholders and the media.

Key Topics of the Chapter

- A fraud is the action of deceiving someone to obtain an unfair or illegal benefit.
- The main types of business frauds are corruption, asset theft, and accounting manipulation.
- Frauds cost companies around 5% of their sales figure. This loss is caused mainly by accounting manipulations.
- Accounting manipulations are done mainly to modify the profit and/or debt.
- Accounts can be modified through accounting manipulations (legal or illegal) and actual transactions (legal or illegal).
- Accounting manipulations have several denominations:

  Creative accounting is the most-used expression in the United Kingdom.

  Earnings management is predominant in the United States and usually refers to legal accounting manipulations that seek to increase or reduce earnings. However, when manipulations are illegal they are called *earnings manipulations*.

  Accounting shenanigans.

  Income smoothing is an earnings management variant that transfers earnings (or losses) from one year to another.

  Big bath is another variant of earnings management that consists in increasing losses (or reducing profits) significantly in a year to reverse them in the future and thus, improve future profits.

REFERENCES

ACCID. (2016). *Ratios sectoriales 2015: Balances de situación, cuentas de resultados y ratios de 166 sectores, Barcelona*.

ACFE. (2016). *The 2016 ACFE Report to the Nations on Occupational Fraud and Abuse*. Austin: Association of Certified Fraud Examiners.

Amat, O., and Blake, J. (1996). *Contabilidad Creativa*. Barcelona: Gestión 2000.

Black, E.L., Sellers, K.F., and Manly, T.S. (1998). Earnings management using asset sales: An international study of countries allowing noncurrent asset revaluation. *Journal of Business Finance & Accounting* (November–December): 1287–1317.

Elvira, O., and Amat, O. (2008). La manipulación contable: Tipología y técnicas. *Partida Doble* 203 (October): 48–59.

Gay, J.M. (2013). Escándalos contables y financieros: de Banesto a Bankia, *Revista de Contabilidad y Dirección* (16): 63–108.

KPMG. (2010). *Informe sobre los delitos económicos y fraude empresarial.*

Laínez, J.A., and Callao, S. (1999). *Contabilidad Creativa.* Madrid: Ed. Civitas.

National Commission on Fraudulent Financial Reporting. (1987). *Report of the National Commission on Fraudulent Financial Reporting.* https://www.coso .org/Documents/NCFFR.pdf.

Paris, J. (2016): *Estudio de las prácticas de alisamiento de resultados. Perfil de la empresa alisadora.* Tesis Doctoral, Universitat Abat Oliba CEU, Barcelona.

PricewaterhouseCoopers. (2016). *Global Economic Crime Survey 2016.* https:// www.pwc.com/gx/en/economic-crime-survey/pdf/GlobalEconomicCrimeSurvey 2016.pdf.

Saurinas, J. (1999). Existe alisamiento del beneficio en las cajas de ahorros españolas. *Moneda y Crédito* (209): 161–193.

Stolowy, H., and Breton, G. (2000). A framework for the classification of accounts manipulations. *Les cahiers de recherche.* Chambre de Commerce et d'industrie de Paris (28 June).

CHAPTER 2

Accounting Fraud: An Ancient Practice

A merchant wanted to know how much two plus two was.
  The accountant, after ensuring no one could hear them, murmured in his ear:
  "How much do you want it to be?"

—Anonymous Venetian

2.1 THE FIRST ACCOUNTING FRAUDS

Recent accounting scandals promote the belief that this is a problem of the nowadays' world, but actually it's an ancient problem and inherent to the human being. As José Saramago (2000) reminds us: "Man is capable of the best and the worst." Accounting fraud exists since the existence of accounting. The first evidence of the existence of accounting is in ancient Mesopotamia, over 4,000 years ago, and it was related to the commerce and the tributes that financed the activity of the temples. From those times are the first accounting records on clay boards or papyruses that informed the profits obtained with the harvests and they were the basis for calculating taxes. From those remote years there is evidence of accounting frauds like the ones mentioned below.

Years later, to avoid these scams, clay tablets or papyruses started being guarded in clay envelopes that weren't opened until they were delivered at the temples.

Centuries later, around 400 BC, in Ancient Egypt, Babylonia, and India, there were control systems of the entrances and exits of stores that were oral, since movements were explained out loud to tribute inspectors. In fact, these controls were the first audits (from Latin *audire*, which means to hear).

ACCOUNTING FRAUDS IN ANCIENT MESOPOTAMIA

Accounting frauds occurred when workers and scribes sent by the temple kept a part of the tribute, after modifying the profits of the harvests. When there were suspicions that the clay tablets or papyruses had been manipulated, it was investigated and if the suspicions were confirmed, the offenders were punished with fines that, according to the Hammurabi Code (from the year 1780 BC), could reach six times the embezzled amount. This code was engraved in a basalt block almost 2.5 meters high and was based in the law of retaliation. In the most serious cases of fraud, the sentences could consist of mutilations or even death. If the fraud was done harming the king, the author should compensate with 30 times the embezzled amount. If the author couldn't pay, he was executed.

Also during those years there were several frauds. For example, in the fourth century BC, over 40 embezzlements of public funds from accounting fraud have been documented in India.

2.2 ACCOUNTING FRAUDS CONTINUE WITH THE DOUBLE ENTRY

Years passed and concepts, accounting techniques, and the quality of information provided improved, but frauds continued. One of the most decisive advances occurred in 1494, when Luca Pacioli published his book *Summa de Arithmetica, Geometria, Proportioni et Proportionalità*, in which he explained the bases of double entry, the accounting system that is still used today. Accounting information has been improving in quality, especially as a reaction to scandals that have been occurring. We can recall, for example, the case of the Dutch East India Company.

Shareholders' complaints, like those that occurred in the Dutch East India Company in 1622, made the authorities force companies to provide information to its shareholders.

These scandals motivated some companies to voluntarily employ auditors to ensure that there were no frauds in the accounts. Thus, for example, from 1880, Scottish and English capitalists who invested in the American stock market sent their auditors to ensure that the balances provided by the companies were reliable.

THE DUTCH EAST INDIA COMPANY

This company, founded in 1602, is considered one of the first multinationals and the first company whose shares were traded in Amsterdam's official stock market. A few years later, significant problems occurred due to bad corporate governance caused by several circumstances. Among them, we can highlight the election of the administrators, since a small group of shareholders, who had over 50% of the capital, elected themselves as administrators and lifetime account supervisors. The rest of the shareholders, who were a few hundred, couldn't participate in the election. Further, the administrators were also great merchants and the company's main customers. Therefore, they had conflicts of interest. Finally, since a shareholder's right for information wasn't regulated, they did not report its accounts to small shareholders. In fact, the first information was provided ten years after its creation, after suffering major losses. The main shareholders, however, did receive information on the company's progress at all times. Later, in 1622, minority shareholders rebelled at the suspicion that the accounts were being manipulated and demanded a review of the accounts and that the results be made public. For this, they designated a few shareholders to ensure that the accounting was accurate. However, these people lacked the time or the knowledge to ensure an effective control of the accounts and the management of the company.

Over the years, these shortcomings improved. The company lived years of glory and in 1669 it had over 150 merchant ships, 40 warships, 50,000 employees and 10,000 soldiers. Most years it distributed dividends. Nevertheless, strong competition from similar companies in other European countries, and the wars with England, wiped out most of their ships and possessions. In 1800 it dissolved.

The Bankruptcy of the South Sea Company

This company, created in 1711, secured the monopoly of all English trade with South America. Shortly after, it started to disclose accounting information that indicated it was obtaining large profits, trading with gold from Peru, which was false because its activities had not yet begun. In less than a year, shares went from being worth 100 pounds

(Continued)

to over 700 pounds. During that time, the company made increases in capital that were subscribed within hours by crazed investors who paid increasingly more money for the shares. Given that the company remained inactive, but had a lot of money as a result of its continuous increases in capital, it started paying dividends to shareholders. Soon after, panic began to spread among investors when news broke that the company's business activities would not start for the time being. Within days the shares dropped 85%. The company ended up going bankrupt without generating any kind of positive result in its operations in America. One of the shareholders who was ruined was Isaac Newton, who lost 20,000 pounds (which today would be worth 268 million pounds) and stated: "I can calculate the movement of stars, but not the madness of men."

The Collapse of the City of Glasgow Bank

The bank was founded in 1839. It specialized in raising deposits to invest in loans and shares in US mining companies. Everything seemed to be going well until mid-1878 when it had 133 offices, financially sound accounts, and paid annual dividends of 12% to its shareholders. On October 2nd of that year, the management announced the closure of the bank. A subsequent investigation proved that it was bankrupt and that the accounts had been forged, as well as the certificates of the valuation of the mining investments that it had in the United States. The banks' leadership was sentenced to prison, but since the shareholders had unlimited responsibility, they had to pay from their pockets the compensation to depositors. 254 of the 1,200 shareholders filed for bankruptcy.

2.3 THE CRASH OF 1929 AND THE OBLIGATION TO AUDIT ACCOUNTS

The obligation to audit accounts and to provide the audit report arrived several decades later, after the stock market crash of 1929. This caused, among other important regulatory changes, that from 1930 onwards in the United States, listed companies would be obliged to report their financial statements and submit them to external auditing by a Certified Public Accountant (CPA). But in 1938, there was another scandal that prompted deeper changes: that of McKesson & Robbins.

THE McKESSON & ROBBINS FRAUD

In 1938 it was discovered that this company had fraudulently inflated its inventory and customers' balances for over 10 years, through fake delivery notes and invoices. From a total of $87 million in assets, McKesson & Robbins forged $10 million of inventory and $9 million of clients' money. These are very high amounts, taking into account the time at which the fraud occurred. The auditors had given their approval to the accounts, since in those years it wasn't mandatory to make a list of physical goods or to confirm the balances with third parties (customers, suppliers, banks, etc.). The circumstances of Philip Musica (the person who perpetrated this fraud) are analyzed in more detail in Chapter 4.

Due to the McKesson & Robbins' scandal, in 1941 the United States Securities and Exchange Commission (SEC) introduced the requirement that auditors include in their work the confirmation of balances with third parties and the physical verification of the existence of tangible assets, as is the case of inventories. Also, auditors would have to send their reports to stockholders.

A few years later, in 1968, there was the scandal of the Bar Chris Construction Corporation. This company had a very significant impairment between the closing date of the year and the date the audit report became public. That is to say, the change occurred immediately after the year's closing date. Therefore, when the auditors gave their approval to the year-end accounts, they didn't say anything regarding the negative events that occurred afterwards.

This led to the audit rules introducing the obligation to evaluate subsequent events that could modify the image offered by the accounts at the closing date.

2.4 REINFORCEMENT OF THE COMMERCIAL LAW AND AUDITING AFTER THE STRING OF SCANDALS OF 2000

Despite the continuous reforms in the regulations, frauds kept occurring. In 2000, coinciding with the burst of the internet bubble, a series of major accounting scandals came to light and, among them, one of the most shocking in history: Enron.

ENRON: FROM MOST ADMIRED COMPANY TO BANKRUPTCY

At the beginning of 2000 Enron was one of the most admired companies in the world and the seventh largest in the United States. It had a turnover of $100,000 million per year and was the largest energy company in the world.

It was also huge in its accounting fraud, which started in 1997, coinciding with the arrival of Jeffrey Skilling, one of Harvard's top MBA graduates. Enron didn't include in its accounts from 1997 to 2000 the accounts corresponding to three thousand subsidiaries established in the Cayman Islands. These companies were financed by bank loans (especially from J.P.Morgan Chase, Wachovia, Credit Suisse, Citigroup, First Boston and Merrill Lynch), which were endorsed by Enron. With these loans, the subsidiaries acquired assets from Enron at above-market prices, thus generating fictitious profits at Enron worth $591 million in four years. In addition, Enron inflated assets and hid debts through its subsidiaries in the Cayman Islands.

When the fraud was discovered, shares went from $90 to $0, and shareholders lost $70,000 million. Soon after, in 2001, the company went bankrupt. 20,000 workers lost their jobs. The managers, who hid the problem until the last moment, had sold all their shares just before the scandal broke out. We will return to this case later.

Enron's bankruptcy occurred soon after the burst of the internet bubble (in 2000) and was followed by other accounting scandals (WorldCom, Global Crossing, Tyco, Xerox, Parmalat, and so on). At that moment, accounting and auditing credibility for corporations was widely questioned around the world. As an example, we recall the statement of Samuel A. DiPiazza, chairman of PwC (2002):

> There is a crisis in the accounting information provided by companies . . . The impact is global . . . it affects stock markets, investors and economies around the world.

Also in 2002, Harvey Pitt, chairman of the SEC, stated:

> Accounting irregularities have been concealed, balances have been inflated . . . it is a blatant fraud perpetrated by those responsible for the companies . . . with the almost absolute mistake of those who had to avoid it, auditors, boards of directors, lawyers and regulators. Everything has failed.

From that moment, major reforms were introduced (Sarbanes–Oxley Act in the United States and modifications in the mercantile and audit laws in many countries). For example, since 2002, the Public Company Accounting Oversight Board (PCAOB) has the responsibility of controlling the quality of the firms that audit listed companies. Big accounting reforms were also undertaken, like the adoption of the International Financial Reporting Standards (IFRS) in many countries.

In 2004, the European Union opted to adopt the IFRS for listed groups. During these years, efforts from regulators as well as companies and accounting users have been very significant.

2.5 WITH THE CRISIS OF 2008, HISTORY REPEATS ITSELF

However, in 2008, with the burst of the housing bubble and subsequent global financial crisis, scandals very similar to those of 2002 were repeated. Each time there is a major crisis, scandals resurface again because many companies' problems emerge (Callao and Jarne, 2010). As in the tale of the naked king from Hans Christian Andersen, the economy starts to falter when the numbers of many companies are no longer what they seemed to be. Let's recall the case of Lehman Brothers.

LEHMAN BROTHERS

In 2008, this global entity of financial services was the protagonist of one of the biggest bankruptcies in the world. Until that moment, it had been able to hide a massive accounting manipulation that consisted in transferring garbage loans from insolvent clients to subsidiaries in the Cayman Islands. Once again, these paradisiacal islands were once more associated to accounting problems. This way, it gave the image of having $50 billion in its treasury, instead of loans that were worth nothing. Therefore, it was concealing multimillion-dollar losses.

Due to this scandal, that caused Lehman's bankruptcy, investors and financial markets started to panic, which was the detonator of a global financial crisis from which many countries still haven't recovered.

Later, we will expand the information on this case.

Surprisingly, successive reforms and increase in all kinds of controls haven't prevented accounting scandals from continuing unabated, especially in recession years. Demerjian et al. (2013) estimated at over 50% the listed companies in the United States reformulated their accounts between the years 2006 and 2009 as a consequence of errors in them. A few years earlier, from 1997 to 2002, in the United States there were 919 listed companies that reformulated their accounts. The main reason for the reformulation was the existence of errors, whether by fraud or not. In the United States, the SEC discovers an average between 100 and 200 cases of accounting fraud per year (Eaglesham and Rapoport 2015). According to the SEC, the main frauds consisted in the mispricing of assets and debts, the incorrect estimation of income and deficiencies in the risk information. As a sign that we are facing a global problem, we recall the worldwide study by Ernst & Young (2013), conducted with surveys of more than 3,000 managers that concludes 42% of managers worldwide believe companies manipulate their accounting.

However, as we have shown, we must bear in mind that a part of the reformulations of accounts are not related to fraud but to errors, as we recall below.

REFORMULATION OF ACCOUNTS IN AN AMERICAN BANK

In 2016, this company corrected its accounts from years 2013 to 2016 (first quarter) due to errors from previous years detected by auditors. There were three types of errors:

1. Incorrect distribution of the amortization of expenses related to the loans throughout the loans life cycle.
2. Estimation of the impairment due to loan default.
3. Discount rate applied in the calculation of the current value of loans.

The reformulation was accepted by the SEC and, in this case, since it implied a higher profit per share in the first trimester of 2016, it caused a rise of 14% in the stock price.

	2013	2014	2015	2016 First quarter
Initially declared earnings per share	+2.01	+2.15	+2.31	0.56
Errors	+0.07	−0.09	−0.01	+0.02
Adjusted earnings per share	+2.08	+2.06	+2.30	+0.58

FIGURE 2.1 Evolution of the earnings per share initially stated, errors and adjusted earnings per share, from 2013 to 2016 (first quarter), of an American bank

Key Topics of the Chapter

- Accounting frauds are not a problem exclusive to the world today. They are as old as accounting, since evidence has been found of accounting frauds of 4,000 years ago.

- Over time, accounting, as well as the demand for transparency and information control, has been improving. First, companies were obliged to keep accounting, then, to inform shareholders, and, subsequently, to audit accounts and improve transparency.

- However, successive reforms and increases in all kinds of controls haven't prevented accounting scandals from continuing unabated, especially in recession years.

- The most common frauds are related to the mispricing of assets and debts, incorrect estimation of income, and deficiencies in risk information.

REFERENCES

Callao, S., and Jarne, J.I. (2010). El impacto de la crisis en la manipulación contable. *Revista de Contabilidad* 14 (2).

Demerjian, P., Lev, B., Lewis, M.F., and McVay, S.E. (2013). Managerial ability and earnings quality. *The Accounting Review* 88(2): 463–498.

DiPiazza, S.A., and Eccles, R.G. (2002). *Building Public Trust. The Future of Corporate Reporting*. New York: Wiley.

Eaglesham, J., and Rapoport, M. (2015). SEC gets busy with accounting inquiries. *Wall Street Journal* (25 January).

Ernst & Young. (2013). *Navigating Today's Complex Business Risks. Fraud Survey 2013*. London: Ernst & Young.

Gironella, E. (1978). La auditoria independiente en los Estados Unidos: Evolución de sus objetivos y técnicas. *Revista Española de Financiación y Contabilidad*, 7(26): 155–182.

Mills, D.Q. (2003). *Wheel, Deal, and Steal: Deceptive Accounting, Deceitful CEOs, and Ineffective Reforms*. Upper Saddle River, NJ: Financial Times Prentice Hall.

Pacioli, L. (1494). *Summa de Arithmetica, Geometria, Proportioni et Proportionalità*. Venice: Paganini.

Saramago, J. (2000). *La caverna*. Madrid: Editorial Alfaguara.

CHAPTER 3

Problems with Legislation and Those Involved in the Financial Information

A balance sheet is inevitably false, because either things are valued for what they have cost, and what they have cost is not generally what they're worth, or we pretend to write them down for what they're worth and, how can we know the value of something we don't know when and at what price we will sell?

—Auguste Detoeuf (1883–1947), founder of Alsthom

3.1 HOW FINANCIAL INFORMATION IS GENERATED

When companies' financial information reaches users (mainly shareholders, credit institutions, and creditors), it has followed a process as the one shown in Figure 3.1. The company's executives prepare the accounts, the board of directors formulates them and the annual general meeting approves them. Auditors also intervene to express their opinion on the reasonableness of the accounts in accordance with current accounting and auditing standards. Finally, the analysts and rating companies that assess and comment on the situation and perspectives of the company also participate. The quality of this process is followed by supervisory agencies.

In regard to the company's executives and the board of directors, there are factors that can condition negatively. The pressure to obtain the expected results is accentuated in recession years and the generalization of incentive systems based on short-term financial results aggravates it. In many companies there are perverse incentive systems that promote actions that can raise the bonus to be received but hurting the company and its stakeholders (customers, workers, shareholders, etc.) in the long term. This

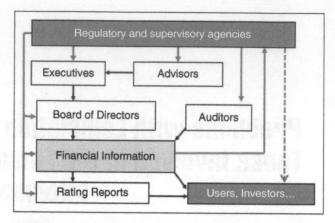

FIGURE 3.1 Agents that intervene in the formulation, approval, control, and diffusion of the financial information

pressure, accompanied by an impairment of ethical standards, can increase the temptation to manipulate accounts and mislead auditors, as well as shareholders and other account users.

3.2 AUDITING OF ACCOUNTS: ESSENTIAL, BUT NOT INFALLIBLE

Auditors of accounts speak out on the reasonableness of companies' financial information. They are a key piece to achieving the highest levels of transparency and reliability, but it must be clear what is expected of an audit of accounts. As stated by Faura (2016):

> *The objective of an audit is to increase the degree of user's trust in the financial statements drawn up by the managers of the companies, by expressing an opinion on whether the financial statements have been prepared, in all material aspects, in accordance with an applicable financial reporting framework. To formulate his opinion, the auditor must have reasonable certainty that the financial statements as a whole are free from material misstatement due to fraud or error. A reasonable certainty is a high degree of assurance, which requires the obtaining of sufficient and adequate Audit evidence to reduce the auditing risk to an acceptably low level, but under no circumstance it supposes absolute certainty ... Those responsible for the government of the entity and the management are the main ones responsible for the prevention and detection of frauds.*

Therefore, the discovery of frauds isn't the main goal in the auditor's job, regardless of whether frauds are discovered during the audit. However, accounts' users usually have a different perception and, therefore, when an accounting scandal breaks out, many wonder: "Where were the auditors?"

This question arises from what is known as the *expectation gap*. This gap is due to the fact that what users expect from accountants and auditors is not the same as what they (accountant and auditors) intend to offer (García Benau 2016). Users expect the annual accounts to inform of the reality of a company, in order to be able to make appropriate decisions. Thus, they expect assets to be valued at prices similar to those of the market. They also want, if the company has a problem or fraud, or could have it in a near future, auditors to warn them well in advance. Instead, auditors and accountants present information that has to reflect the true image of the economic and financial situation of the company. But by true image accountants and auditors don't present the reality, but that which is derived from the application of accounting standards, even if they deviate from reality. For this reason, they can say that accounts that do not include most of the intangibles, or real estate valuations at market price, which may also vary according to the accounting standards of each country, reflect the true image.

This expectation gap goes back a long way. As an example, let's remember the case of Kingston Cotton Mills Co.

It is possible that in the next few years the expectation gap will be reduced, since recent changes in audit reports further clarify the auditor's responsibility regarding accounting fraud.

Another relevant aspect is the quality of the audit work. In the United States, the Public Company Accounting Oversight Board (PCAOB) controls the quality of the companies that audit listed companies. To do this, it reviews between 300 and 400 audit reports each year. These reviews detect between 15% and 40% of audit reports with deficiencies (Walworth 2015). These deficiencies are related to the evaluation of internal control, the accounting estimates, and samplings.

However, most audit reports don't generate problems. As an example, let's remember that in Spain, 62,000 audits are done every year, carried out by almost 1,200 auditing companies and around 6,000 auditors. Of this, a little more than 20 present problems that ultimately lead to sanctions from the supervisor (Institute of Accounting and Audit of Accounts).

On the other hand, there have been many cases where a warning signal on erroneous accounts was given by the auditors. In Chapter 11, for example, we will look back on the case of Afinsa and *Fórum Filatélico*, where auditors gave clear signals two years before bankruptcy. The same occurred with *Nueva Rumasa*.

THE ROLE OF THE AUDITOR AND THE BANKRUPTCY OF KINGSTON COTTON MILLS CO.

Kingston Cotton Mills Co. was a textile company created in 1845. However, the moment in which Kingston Cotton Mills Co. was created wasn't the best, since the British Government had raised, in 1843, the prohibition of exporting textile machinery to other countries. At that moment, the competitive advantage that British cotton companies had disappeared. Despite that, Kingston Cotton Mills Co. started to operate, producing and exporting to many countries, especially the United States. However, the American Civil War affected it, generating great losses due to lost goods and uncollected sales. When the war was over, the company returned to work but things would no longer be as before. In 1894, when it had 1,300 employees, the company went bankrupt due to being unable to repay its loans. Until that moment, auditors' reports had reflected that the company was doing well and there was nothing to suggest that it actually generated losses. Later, it was revealed that the auditor approved the stock balance in the warehouses without doing a physical inventory, since he only had a certificate from the company that declared a value for the warehouse, which was then shown to be very inflated.

The shareholders sued management and the auditors. Nevertheless, the auditors were declared not guilty in the trial that ended in 1896. Judge Lord Lopes, exonerating the auditors, stated:

"An auditor isn't obliged to be a detective ... it's a guard dog, not a bloodhound."

In any case, there are numerous cases of accounting fraud that have not been detected by the auditors. According to a study by Beasley, Carcello, Hermanson, and Neal (2013), in 55% of the accounting frauds produced in the United States between 1998 and 2010, audit reports had a favorable opinion and without reservations.

On some occasions, auditors have made mistakes by not detecting frauds committed by the managers. However, in most cases, they were also deceived by the managers and suffer the consequences.

ARTHUR ANDERSEN DECLARED NOT GUILTY

We have already referred to the Enron scandal, which caused, among other consequences, the end of Arthur Andersen, one of the five biggest auditing companies, ending a successful 89-year career. In 2002 the jury found Arthur Andersen guilty of obstruction of justice. In particular, it was accused of ordering its employees, in 2001, to destroy documents related to the Enron fraud.

Although the audit firm always denied these accusations, the jury's decision caused its disappearance. At that time, it had tens of thousands of employees and was internationally renowned. Nevertheless, in 2005, the United States Supreme Court nullified the sentence and found Arthur Andersen not guilty of the crimes it had been imputed. According to the Supreme Court, the culprits were the managers. It isn't the first time the auditor ends up paying for the sins of unethical managers, who deceive everyone, including its auditors.

The problem with Arthur Andersen's exculpatory sentence is that it came too late, as the audit firm had already disappeared.

In any case, Arthur Andersen's three main auditors, who participated in the Enron audit, lost their license to audit.

A problem that plays against is the downward pressure on audit fees, caused by the high competition and the pressure from clients who ask for lower prices. This could in some cases promote impairment in the quality of the auditor's work.

3.3   ANALYSTS AND RATING AGENCIES

Financial and investment analysts can also notify in time when there are problems. However, sometimes analysts work in organizations that operate as intermediaries. In this case, there may be a conflict of interest; for there to be more business of buying and selling, the analysts' opinion must be favorable. It isn't surprising, therefore, that most analysis reports recommend buying the shares of the company analyzed.

MERRILL LYNCH'S RECOMMENDATIONS

After the 2002 wave of accounting scandals, New York's attorney general showed that Merrill Lynch recommended to their clients buying stocks from companies that were internally classified as garbage. In the end, in order to avoid trial, it accepted to compensate affected clients with $100 million.

A surprising fact is that in the United States, more than 70% of companies exceed profit estimates agreed by analysts. According to Lev (2016), this high percentage is due either to the fact that a large part of analysts' estimates are altered, or to the fact that companies manipulate a lot their accounts. Either explanation is cause for worry.

THE ROLE OF SOME ANALYSTS IN THE ENRON SCANDAL

Frequently, analysts complain they get pressured, even by their own company, to issue favorable reports on the companies they analyze. On August 23, 2001, an analyst at the BNP Paribas investment Bank was fired, who had issued a few days earlier a negative recommendation concerning Enron. He was the first analyst to issue an opinion questioning Enron's benefits, which in fact was accurate taking into account the company's actual impairment that became public a few weeks later.

Afterward, on May 21, 2002, Merrill Lynch came to an agreement with the New York prosecutor to pay a fine of $110 million to avoid going to trial for misleading recommendations to investors. It also pledged to separate the pay of its analysts from the progress of the investment banking business and to set the incentives based on the accuracy of their analysis (Nieto, 2002).

It is also key the role of rating agencies. The increase of financial information and the rise in its complexity explain why rating agencies are increasingly more necessary. Investors need to know quickly issuers' ability to pay. Unfortunately, the crisis of 2008 showed that the opinions of rating agencies aren't foolproof. Companies that had until recently received very favorable

FIGURE 3.2 Evolution of Lehman Brothers quotation (dollars) and rating
Source: Bloomberg.

ratings from rating agencies went bankrupt (Lehman Brothers, for example). Figure 3.2 shows the evolution of Lehman Brothers' price from September 2007 until its bankruptcy in 2008. The rating from Standard & Poors was A+ until June 2, 2008, when it was lowered to A. After the bankruptcy, the rating became Default (suspension of payments), but it was already too late for investors who had trusted the company.

One of the rating agencies' issues that generate questions is the fact that its owners are big investment funds, especially from the United States. Also, rating agencies are hired by the same institutions they must rate, so their independence can be questioned. Another problem is the lack of competition in this field, and the resulting existence of an oligopoly. Apart from Standard & Poors, Moodys, and Fitch, they almost monopolize the global-rating market (Moody, for example, makes around 40% of ratings worldwide). There are other agencies, such as AM Best (United States), Veda Advantage (Australia), Dominion Bond Rating Service (Canada), Japan Credit Rating Agency (Japan), Clasificadora de Riesgo Humphreys (Chile), and Companhia Portuguesa de Rating (Portugal). Most of these agencies specialize in more local financial markets.

An example of the influence of rating agencies is the opinion of Thomas Friedman, a journalist for the *New York Times*: "In fact, you could almost say that we live again in a two-superpower world. There is the U.S. and there is Moody's."

Oligopolies often generate inconvenience, like forcing increase in prices and reducing the quality of the products offered. These problems contribute to the increase of doubts regarding the usefulness of valuations, and recently the creation of public rating agencies has been demanded. However, these would have an additional conflict of interest for its lack of independence from governments.

For reasons such as the ones mentioned, in the European Union there have been improvements, since the agencies have become subject to a system of registration and supervision of their methods that has been entrusted to the European Supervisory Markets Authorities (ESMA). The new regulation consists of ensuring that agencies have enough organizational means to perform its task, and that its internal organization eliminates, or at least palliates, the indicated conflicts of interest. Another important aspect is that agencies must give transparency to the models used for the determination of the ratings. In addition, the agency must ensure that the information entered in the models is all the relevant to make the qualification and has not been selected basely. Finally, agencies must give more information about the changes in classification, so that they are more justified than they have been so far. All these changes in the regulation may contribute to improve some of the existing problems, although criticism of the oligopolistic position and conflicts of interest continue to occur.

3.4 REGULATORS AND THE LIMITATIONS OF ACCOUNTING REGULATIONS

Regulators have the mission of producing good regulations and supervisors are responsible for monitoring that the rules are complied with. As already indicated, in years of recession there are usually accounting scandals worldwide that evidence both problems of bad regulation as well as bad supervision. For this reason, it is common that in each economic recession period new regulations are approved in an attempt to prevent the reoccurrence of frauds.

In the United States, the accounting standards are done by the FASB (Financial Accounting Standards Board) and the supervision by the SEC, although there are also other organizations, such as the PCAOB that, as we have already mentioned, supervise audit reports from listed companies.

A relevant part of the manipulations is due to the limitations of financial information:

- **Acquisition price:** In many countries' accounting standards, the principle of prudence and of acquisition price prevails, indicating that assets must be valued at the lowest price between the acquisition price and the market price. Also, the acquisition price reduces with the corresponding accumulated depreciations. This means that in those companies that have assets, especially properties acquired many years ago, these have a book value that is very far from the reality. This problem has been partially solved with the adoption of the International Financial Reporting Standards which allows accounting for assets such as properties at market price, even though its acquisition price is lower. This is a partial solution since most companies and countries, although they have adopted the International Financial Reporting Standards (IFRS), continue giving precedence to the acquisition price, even though the market price is much higher.

■ **International accounting differences:** Accounting rules change a lot depending on the country in question. This explains why the same transaction may have different impacts in the accounts.

For example, in Germany properties are valued at acquisition price, minus the corresponding depreciations. On the other hand, in the IFRS it is allowed to value properties at market price. In other countries, especially in South America, companies adjust their accounts and, therefore, the real estate, according to the inflation produced.

Areas where there are big differences between countries are the assets valuation criteria, the treatment of income and expenses, depreciation and provisions, stock options, research and development, the recognition of contingencies, in pension plans, operations in foreign currency, consolidation rules, and the criteria to estimate future transactions, among others. In order to evaluate the impact of these differences, we can see an example based on an European company to which the accounting standards of several countries have been applied to the transactions carried out during a year (see Figure 3.3).

It is true that in recent years the adoption of the IFRS has been spreading all over the world, which is favoring a process of convergence between many countries' accounting rules. In any case, although progress has been made in the international accounting harmonization, there is still a long way to go.

■ **Intangibles:** The pillars for modern accounting were designed a few centuries ago when companies' most important assets were the tangible assets, such as buildings, machines, and inventory. Nowadays, in many companies an important part of their value is in the so-called intangibles,

Standards Applied to a Company's Transactions	Earnings before taxes
International Financial Reporting Standards (IFRS)	100
US Generally Accepted Accounting Principles (US GAAP)	76

FIGURE 3.3 Alterations in a company's earnings with IFRS and US GAAP
Source: Author's own work. Each country's most common accounting criteria have been applied to the transactions done during the year of 2014. The result is considered according to the IFRS criteria as base 100.

such as brands, employees' know-how, distribution network, clients, technology, and others. Most of these assets aren't included in the balance sheet and this greatly explains the difference between a company's book value and its market value. In October 2016, for example, the market value of listed companies in the United States exceeded by 2.9 times the book value for values included in the Standard & Poor's index.

■ **Regulations' complexity:** With the new accounting standards approved after the Enron scandal in 2000, an additional problem has appeared: the complexity of many assessment rules in most countries makes understanding difficult for accountants and users of accounting (Marín and Anton 2010).

All these problems make it questionable nowadays the usefulness of companies' accounting and financial information. Lev (2016), for example, states: "Companies' financial information isn't useful to make the investment and financing decisions of the twenty-first century."

But the reforms in the accounting standards, despite its high costs and complexity, haven't allowed generating more useful information for decision-making. Wang and Yu (2015) demonstrate, with a study of 44 countries, that the successive accounting reforms haven't provided more relevant information to accounting users.

EXAMPLE OF IMPACT OF THE ACCOUNTING STANDARD APPLIED

It is a case based on a real company that has prepared the accounts based on two different accounting standards (IFRS and US GAAP). Since it is a company that has items such as properties, financial leasing and financial instruments, which are treated differently in each standard, the annual accounts change significantly.

Main Ratios	IFRS	US GAAP
Current ratio (Current Assets/Current Liabilities)	1.35	1.15
Debt (Liabilities/Assets)	0.53	0.71
Assets Turnover (Sales/Assets)	0.89	1.32
Return on Equity (Net Earnings/Equity)	0.10	0.19

From the previous information, it's clear that in this case the accounts with IFRS are the ones that give a better image (more liquidity and less debt). The accounts prepared with US GAAP, on the other hand, are those that show more asset turnover and profitability.

This exercise shows how the accounting standards can make a company able to offer a very different image depending on the accounting standards applied.

3.5 ROLE OF THE MEDIA

Sometimes, the interest of the media for not informing or misinforming about the reality of companies, have been questioned. In many accounting scandals some media have played an unclear role. For example, the reporter Dan Scotto from the *Wall Street Journal* was fired for comparing Enron to the naked emperor, according to Elliott and Schroth (2003). In Spain, you can go through the newspaper archives to see the exquisite treatment that most media gave to Nueva Rumasa until a few days before the outbreak of the scandal. Perhaps it is an isolated case, but in this scandal many media refused to publish articles that warned about the problems before the scandal broke out. It was media (newspaper, radio, television) that benefited from the continuous publicity campaigns that were done until a little before Nueva Rumasa went into bankruptcy.

Key Topics of the Chapter

- Many accounting frauds are related by aspects that affect those involved in the creation of accounting information, its control or its diffusion:
  - Impairment of ethical standards and perverse incentive systems for managers and members of boards of directors.
  - Auditors' mistakes, although in the vast majority of audits there are no problems.
  - Conflicts of interest and mistakes from analysts, rating agencies and media.
  - Problems of bad regulation or errors from regulators and supervisors.
- Another problem is caused by the difference of expectations between what accounting users expect (reliability and adequacy to the reality of the accounts) and what accountants/auditors really deliver (compliance with accounting standards, although it may be far from the reality).

- The reliability of the financial information is also affected by legislative problems, such as the preeminence of the acquisition price (although far from the real value of assets), the international accounting differences, the insufficient recognition of intangibles, legal accounting manipulations and the increasing complexity of accounting regulations.

- For reasons as those mentioned above, the usefulness of corporate financial reporting for decision making, which is the main objective of accounting, is often questioned.

REFERENCES

Amat, O. (2002). Reflexiones y propuestas sobre los problemas de la información contable, *Economistas (93)*.

Beasley, M., Carcello, J., Hermanson, D., and Neal, T. (2013). *An Analysis of Alleged Auditor Deficiencies in SEC Fraud Investigations: 1998–2010*. Center for Audit Quality.

DiPiazza, S., and Eccles, R.G. (2002). *Building Public Trust. The Future of Corporate Reporting*. New York: Wiley.

Elliot, A.L., and Schroth, R.J. (2003). *Cómo mienten las empresas*. Barcelona: Gestión 2000.

Faura, D. (2016). El papel del auditor externo en la detección de fraudes. *Revista de Contabilidad y Dirección* (23): 97–111.

García Benau, M.A. (2016). Las expectativas de la auditoría y el fraude. *Revista de Contabilidad y Dirección* (23).

Lev, B. (2016). *The End of Accounting and the Path Forward for Investors and Managers*. Hoboken, NJ: Wiley.

Marín, S., and Antón, M.A. (2010). Información financiera: Experiencias de un año de aplicación de la nueva normativa. *Revista de Contabilidad y Dirección* (10).

Nieto, A.B. (2002). Los inversores presentan demandas para ser indemnizados. *CincoDías* (22 May): 29.

Túa, J. (1985). Algunas precisiones adicionales en torno al principio de imagen fiel. *Técnica Contable* (December): 441–484.

Walworth, W. (2015). "Auditing the auditor: Insights from PCAOB inspection reports." Blog post, June 9. https://www.gaapdynamics.com/insights/blog/2015 /06/09/auditing-the-auditor-insights-from-pcaob-inspection-reports/.

Wang, J., and Yu, W. (2015), The information content of stock prices, legal environment, and accounting standards. *European Accounting Review* (24): 490.

CHAPTER 4

Why Are Accounts Manipulated?

Fraud is the daughter of greed.

—Jonathan Gash

4.1 MOTIVATION, OPPORTUNITY, AND RATIONALIZATION

Those who manipulate accounts do it for multiple reasons, but to understand the process that leads to the existence of these frauds is illustrative the so-called Triangle of Fraud (Cressey 1980). This is a model (see Figure 4.1) that explains the three factors that, when they coincide in time, lead to the commission of fraud. The criminologist Donald Cressey formulated his triangle theory after interviewing over 300 prisoners jailed for having committed several offenses. From the interviews' results, he identified the circumstances that coincide in most offenses.

- **Motivation:** The need or pressure that encourages interest in defrauding. Some examples of motivations that exert pressure to defraud are:
  - Sales and profit decrease and there is an interest in hiding this decline from bankers or shareholders.
  - Paying fewer taxes.
  - A company that will be sold, or will start listing in the stock market, and wants to offer better figures.
  - A company that has to make an employment regulation or has to ask for subsidies and wants to offer worse figures.
  - A manager who wants the profits to be higher to receive a higher variable compensation.
- **Opportunity:** A situation that allows defrauding with a low risk level. The existence of opportunities makes it easier for frauds to occur. As they say in Latin America: "En arca abierta, el justo peca" ("When the chest is open, the just sins"). The English equivalent could be: "Deep down

FIGURE 4.1   The Triangle of Fraud (Cressey, 1980)

we are all thieves," which means that when there is an opportunity, even a person who has no intention of defrauding, may do it.

Examples of situations that provide opportunities for fraud include:
- A company with poor control system.
- An unaudited company or with an inadequate auditor.
- A company with corporate governance problems.
- **Rationalization:** The mental frame that justifies a person committing fraud. Most frauds are committed by normal people who don't see themselves as criminals. They believe they commit fraud because they have a justified cause. The rationalization explains why many people who commit fraud feel good about themselves and don't regret their bad behavior. Examples of events that could justify the rationalization that pushes towards fraud:
  - A company that needs a loan and deceives to avoid firing employees or closing.
  - An executive who commits fraud because he has a feeling of superiority that makes him believe that company rules don't apply to him.
  - An employee who steals to compensate for his low wages, which he considers unfair.
  - An employee that steals because he sees that the management also commits fraud.
  - People who consider licit deceiving because they have Robin Hood syndrome and consider themselves poor, so deceiving the rich (whether shareholders or bankers, for example) is an act of justice (Zayas 2016).
  - In the case of income smoothing, those who do manipulations tend to think they don't harm anyone.

Thus, according to the Triangle of Fraud, fraud is committed when there is a motivation for it, there is the opportunity, and it is considered to be a justified action.

Let's take a look at some real cases of accounting fraud that can be related to the factors that explain the existence of frauds.

Medco: Fictitious Sales Motivated by the IPO (Initial Public Offering)

Medco is a subsidiary of Merck, which in 2012 was about to do an IPO (a circumstance that could be a motivation to embezzle). During the previous three years, Medco posted $12.4 billion in sales that never existed. This practice didn't have an impact in the earnings since the fictitious sales were accompanied by purchases, also fictitious, for the same amount. These were charges that pharmacies made directly to their customers and whose amounts were not reverted to Merck. However, it posted a sale to the pharmacy, accompanied by a purchase for the same amount, also to the pharmacy. Thus, the net impact on Merck's income statement was zero. This posting allowed Merck to report a higher sales figure.

Opportunity and Motivation in the False Accounting of a Credit Institution

A credit institution that went bankrupt in 2009 had to be intervened and nationalized. The bailout of the company demanded the injection of public money worth 9 million euros.

In 2016, the court sentenced several managers to two years in prison. According to the judge's ruling, the manipulation consisted in not accounting for the provisions required by the financial supervisor. This allowed declaring in 2008 a profit, when actually the company was generating losses. The manipulation was done at a time when the company was negotiating its merger with another company. This circumstance can explain what happened from the motivation point of view. Had the high losses been known, the merger would probably not have taken place and, certainly, they would have immediately lost depositors and clients. Also, the financial supervisor's report showed that in the company existed serious control deficiencies, which could be an indication of opportunity.

The 2015 Accounting Scandal in Toshiba

In the summer 2015, the president and seven senior managers of the Japanese giant Toshiba resigned after it was revealed they had inflated the earnings in $1.2 million during the period of 2009–2014.

There were several types of frauds. One of them consisted of Toshiba selling more components than necessary to suppliers to whom it outsourced the assembly of products. These sales raised Toshiba's

(Continued)

earnings, and simultaneously increased supplier's stock balance. Another fraud was done posting lower costs in long-term projects.

The fraud had a clear motivation: the president set very difficult goals to achieve and the company's culture made it seem that orders couldn't be disobeyed. In addition, the variable remuneration depended on the achievement of these goals. What's more, characteristics of the organization facilitated the opportunity to do the manipulation because the three members of the auditing committee didn't have accounting knowledge. Also, the internal audit department devoted itself to do consulting for other departments, but it didn't perform control tasks. Therefore, those who had to control, didn't.

The fraud was revealed after an investigation by the Japanese stock exchange supervisor who later forced the company to improve their control systems under the threat that if it didn't, it would be excluded from the stock market.

4.2 THE DOOR TO FRAUD

After the formulation of the Triangle of Fraud, other authors have proposed additional circumstances to understand why frauds occur. These circumstances are related to the profile of the people who commit frauds:

- **Ability:** The skills of the people who commit frauds (Wolfe and Hermanson, (2004). This means taking into account the skills the fraudster needs to have to commit the fraud. The elements that explain a person having the ability to commit fraud could be:
  - Training (level of education, computer skills, financial engineering, accounting, etc.).
  - Experience.
  - Contact network.
  - Position in the company. For example, certain positions allow intervening in contracts, in the formulation of accounts, and so on. According to Beasley (1996), CEOs and/or general directors intervene in 70% of accounting frauds.
- **Arrogance:** Arrogant people lack humility and they feel superior to everyone else. It is a person's excessive pride in relation to himself that makes him believe and demand more privileges than he has a right to. Arrogant people can be told apart by:
  - An excess of luxury.
  - Narcissism.

- Haughtiness.
- Aggressiveness.
- Excessive exposure to media.
- They criticize behind their backs those they don't like.
- They are cruel with their enemies.
- They lie and cheat often, even on minor issues, like playing cards or practicing sports.
- They get mad, overreacting when someone damages their public image.
- They usually don't acknowledge mistakes and when they make a mistake, they don't apologize.

    Arrogance explains why some people have unlimited greed and the feeling of impunity by believing that company rules don't affect them (Crowe, 2010).
- **Intentions of the fraudster:** Depending on the intention we can differentiate between an accidental fraud committed by someone who didn't necessarily have the intention to do it and the fraud committed by a predator who is fully willing at the moment of committing the fraud (Kranacher et al., 2010). In the latter case we are dealing with a person without any ethical commitment.

    In the case of accounting manipulation, there can be cases when there wasn't the intention to embezzle, but it was rather a mistake. This type of situation can be proven when the company itself immediately recognizes the mistake and corrects it, reformulating the accounts or exposing it in the report and the statement of changes in equity. In all other cases, it is more likely intentional manipulations.

JÉROME KERVIEL'S ABILITY IN THE FRAUD OF SOCIÉTÉ GÉNÉRAL

Société Général lost 4.9 million euros as a result of a series of fraudulent operations performed by Jérome Kerviel, a market operator.

The fraudulent operations consisted of:

- The annotation and subsequent cancelation of 947 accounting notes of fictitious operations. The goal was to manipulate the calculations of risk analysis and valuations.
- Posting 115 cross-selling and buying operations (for the exact same amount) that had the aim to transfer results to the year he

(Continued)

wanted them reflected. For example, in March 2007 he posted the purchase of 2,266,500 shares from the company SolarWorld for 63 euros and, simultaneously, registered the sale of the same number of shares at the price of 53 euros. This enabled him to generate a fictitious loss of 22.7 million euros.

There are cases in which the motivation isn't the fraudster's prosperity, but other types of motivation. For example, in this fraud, Jérome Kerviel didn't pursue wealth for himself, but wanted to gain social recognition (Baker et al., 2016). Kerviel, who had humble origins, wanted to gain notoriety through improving the bank's profits.

Without a doubt, Kerviel had special skills since, in addition to knowing financial techniques, he had previously worked as an internal auditor. Thus, he knew how to elude the controls that the internal audit department was doing. He also had extensive computer skills.

ENRON: SYNONYM OF ARROGANCE

Once again, we talk about Enron. As McLean (2001) wrote in *Fortune* magazine: "Arrogance is the most used word to describe Enron … They began with arrogance, followed with greed, deceits and financial schemes." In the lobby of Enron's headquarters there was a banner that read: "The World's Leading Company." This banner replaced the previous that read "The World's Leading Energy Company," which was already considered by Enron's board too modest. Over six consecutive years, Enron was nominated by *Fortune* magazine the most innovative company among the most-admired companies.

Jeff Skilling, CEO of Enron, was notorious for his arrogance. He often stated, "There are two types of people: those who succeed and those who don't." He had a reputation for hanging up the phone on reporters when they asked questions he didn't like. The company stood out for its pride (it considered itself the best company in the world), excess of luxuries (private jets, impressive parties), contemptuous treatment to journalists who questioned their achievements, and so on.

Another example of the profile of these characters is that, shortly before the scandal broke out, the executives forbade their employees from selling their Enron shares and, therefore, they were ruined. In contrast, top management did sell its shares (registering huge profits) before the company collapsed.

In addition, there were aspects related to the motivation to manipulate—it had a very aggressive variable remuneration system for managers. The bonus was based on an estimation of the value of the company that was done based on internal estimates that overestimated the contracts that were made. This pushed many managers to inflate contracts. In 2001, a few months before its collapse, Enron paid $680 million to 140 executives. President Kenneth Lay received 67.4 million dollars and Jeff Skilling, CEO, received $41.8 million. In addition, the company did a ranking of employees and those on the bottom 20% were automatically dismissed.

There were also symptoms related to opportunity: the company had thousands of subsidiaries in the Cayman Islands and most members of the board of directors were chosen by the president.

In the end, Jeffrey Skilling was sentenced to 24 years in prison; Andrew Fastow received a sentence of six years in prison. The president, Ken Lay, died a few weeks before the judge's sentence was known, which was going to be 45 years in jail. His funeral was attended by then-president of the United States George Bush.

THE PREDATOR PROFILE OF PHILIP MUSICA

Philip Musica was the last chairman of McKesson & Robbins (a company that went bankrupt in 1939 after a big fraud, as explained in Chapter 2). He was born in 1884 in Naples. As Mock (2004) explains, Philip emigrated at the age of 7 with his family to the United States and grew up in the Mulberry Bend Neighborhood in Lower East Side in Manhattan, a neighborhood where the most violent gangs of New York proliferated. At the age of 14, he left school on his mother's orders to help in the creation of a family business that imported and commercialized food products. At 25, Philip was sentenced to a year in prison for bribing customs inspectors who allowed him to declare fewer products and thus reduce the payment of tariffs. At his mother's advice, Philip kept a double accounting, which he used to hide part of his purchases and sales. Philip incriminated himself, absolving his mother and brothers. In prison, he deceived the authorities by saying he had a degree in accounting, which enabled him to work in the administrative department.

He served only 5 of the 12 months he had been sentenced to because the American President William Howard Taft exonerated him

(Continued)

for unknown causes. Then he created, with his family, the US Hair Company, a company that produced hair extensions. At 18 months, the company was listed in one of New York's stock markets and got $3 million from investors in its IPO. It also got bank financing. Philip and his family lived in an ostentatiously luxurious way. However, shortly afterwards police discovered that most of the company's operations were invented and that it was a massive fraud. His mother escaped to Naples. Philip and his siblings were arrested when they tried to escape to Panama by ship. They had suitcases filled with money and jewelry. Again, Philip incriminated himself to release his mother and brothers from all responsibility. He spent less time than anticipated in prison because he became an informer, reporting his fellow inmates.

When Philip left prison, he changed his name (and hairstyle) and was renamed Bill Johnson. He spent a few years working as an investigator at the New York Attorney General's Office. Despite doing very well on the job of pursuing criminals, he was fired when his criminal record was discovered.

He then changed his name again and called himself Frank Costa. With his brothers he created Adelphi Pharmaceuticals that produced hair tonics. In the years of the Prohibition, which banned the production and sale of alcohol, he got the government to authorize him to purchase 20,000 liters of alcohol to produce the tonics. In reality, the company didn't produce the tonics but resold the alcohol. During those years, he stole the wife of a worker, whom he had recently gotten jailed, after accusing him of crimes he hadn't committed.

Shortly after he changed his name again to Dr. Frank Donald Coster (and, once again, he changed his hairstyle) and created another company (Girard & Company) that sold hair tonics. In 1925 it started listing in the New York Stock Exchange and a year later he acquired a centenary company (McKesson & Robbins) that was going through serious difficulties. Afterwards, he created a subsidiary in Canada, without content, but through which, supposedly, it carried out many operations. Its warehouses were empty and were kept to give the appearance that what the company informed in its accounts was real, but in practice it forged the majority of its contracts, purchases, shipments, and sales.

The fraud was discovered when the board of McKesson asked Coster to reduce the excessive inventory by $2 million to reduce the excessive debt and generate cash. Coster responded suggesting to request a $3 million loan. As a result of this, McKesson's treasurer became suspicious. When he first questioned Coster, all he got were evasive answers. After several investigations, he discovered what was happening with the Canadian subsidiary and also discovered that Coster had stolen $3 million from the company. When the accountant reported him to the shareholders and to the police, the company went bankrupt. 13,500 shareholders lost $100 million.

Dr. Frank Donald Coster was accused and released on bail. Shortly after, in a fingerprint control, an employee of the New York Attorney General discovered that Dr. Frank Donald Coster was actually William Johnson (the name he used after his first stay in prison). The prosecutor decided to revoke the bail and incarcerate him. When the police went to get him at his house, on December 16th, 1938, Musica/Johnson/Costa/Coster committed suicide. He left a four-page letter explaining that he had been a victim of Wall Street's pillaging and blackmails.

From the above we can conclude this wasn't an occasional fraudster, but a predator, a person who plunders systematically. Before his last fraud was discovered, he was a highly respected person and was even nominated by the Republican Party as a candidate for the US presidency, an offer he declined, claiming personal obligations.

In a case like the one above, what is surprising is that a person can go on repeating so many frauds and investors repeatedly fall for it. As the old saying goes, "Man is the only animal that trips twice over the same stone." For those who think the previous case is an isolated incident and that it wouldn't happen nowadays, remember the history of Rumasa (a company intervened by the Spanish government in 1983) and what happened with Nueva Rumasa (a company that went insolvent 2011).

Given that the last three characteristics that have been proposed (ability, arrogance, and intention) refer to the fraudster's profile, we propose to include them in a more integrated model that include all four variables and that we can call the door to fraud (see Figure 4.2).

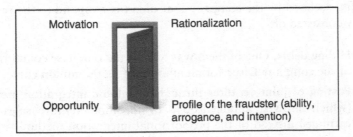

FIGURE 4.2 The door to fraud

We'll use these four main variables from Chapter 8 when we analyze the warning signs that help to detect fraud.

THE ROYAL AHOLD SCANDAL

Royal Ahold is a Dutch multinational of the distribution sector founded in 1887 by Albert Heijn and was first listed on the stock market in 1948.

In 1989, it designed a strategic plan that aimed at being the world leader in sales, surpassing the two giants, Walmart and Carrefour. This meant doubling sales every five years. They also had the goal of increasing earnings each year by 15% (10% with organic growth and 5% through acquisitions). Royal Ahold's strategy was based on the growth through joint ventures at 50% with other companies. The main joint ventures were ICA (Sweden), Disco (Argentina), Bompreço (Brazil), and Paiz (Central America).

Another measure was to compensate the executives with stock options. This meant that it went from the 150 executives in 1987 who were in this system to 6,700 people in 2001. This incentive system, which also included members of the board, was based on the increase of share prices rather than the generation of value for shareholders. A common practice was for directors to sell shares immediately after receiving them.

From 1990 to 2003, Royal Ahold received the award for best company listed in the Netherlands seven times.

The manipulations occurred between 2000 and 2002, when the company operated over 5,155 supermarkets in 27 countries, with over 280,000 employees. The goal of the manipulations was to obtain numbers that didn't disappoint the analysts that followed the company's shares.

The accounting embezzlements were done to hide the growth and profits declared by the company that didn't correspond to the reality. They consisted of:

- **Hiding debts.** One of them was to hide the purchase commitment of the company Disco for an amount of 2,500 million euros.

- **Posting of joint ventures through the global integration method** (which allowed adding 100% of the joint venture sales and earnings) instead of the proportional integration method (which was the one it had to apply and only allows adding the percentage of sales and earnings according to the percentage of shares in the joint-venture's capital, which was 50% maximum). This way they artificially increased sales worth 24,800 million euros. The fraud consisted of showing auditors comfort letters that said the final decision of the joint ventures, in case of disagreement, corresponded to Royal Ahold. In reality, they also had other secret letters that clearly stated that Royal Ahold didn't have real control of these joint ventures and, therefore, they invalidated the comfort letters. These secret letters were hidden from the auditor Deloitte Touche, which was deceived.

- **The profits of the American subsidiary had been inflated.** For this, they overestimated incentives that suppliers had to pay them for reaching certain purchase volumes.
- **Fraudulent capitalization of expenses** in the Argentinian subsidiary Disco.
- **Unwise estimates of debts in relation to pensions** to reduce expenses and reduce the debt.
- **Postings of financial leasing as operating leasing,** to reduce indebtedness.

The scandal was discovered in 2002 when associates from different joint ventures made public the secret letters saying Royal Ahold didn't report correctly in its accounts, basically referring to purchase agreements and the effective control of the joint ventures.

When the scandal broke out, the president and the consultants announced their intention of buying more of Royal Ahold shares, but it was already too late. However, only the president and two other executives kept the promise to buy shares.

The annual accounts for 2000, 2001, and 2002 had to be adjusted (see Figure 4.3).

Due to the scandal, Royal Ahold's shares dropped (see Figure 4.4) and Standard & Poors reduced its rating from BBB to junk bond.

Royal Ahold's problems go back to 1992, when Cees van der Hoeven, who was the CFO, replaced the founder of the company as CEO. Once appointed CEO, Cees van der Hoeven kept the position of CFO. In a few years he replaced most of the managers and members of the board of directors, installing loyal people. The majority of the members of the board didn't have time to exert control functions. For example, Henny de Ruiter (president of the Supervision Committee) exercised the same position in 17 other companies. Other members of

(Continued)

	2000	2001	2002 (until third quarter)
Declared Earnings	**+1,116**	**+1,113**	**+388**
Income from incentives from suppliers	−103	−215	−269
Rest of the manipulations (annulment of the global consolidation, erroneous capitalization of expenses, and other manipulations)	−93	−148	−72
Adjusted earnings (are the earnings after the manipulations are annulled)	**+920**	**+750**	**+47**
Impact of the manipulation in the earnings % Manipulations/Adjusted earnings	21%	48%	625%

FIGURE 4.3 Evolution of the declared earnings, manipulations, and adjusted earnings at Royal Ahold in 2001 and 2002
Source: http://www.jaarverslag.com/assets/reports/JaarverslagCOM_Ahold_ Jaarverslag_2002.pdf.

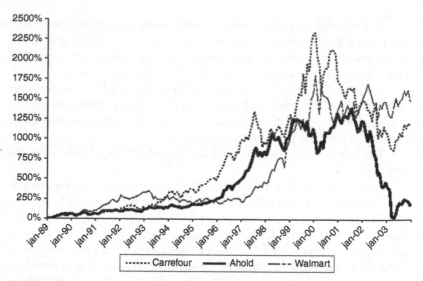

FIGURE 4.4 Evolution of Royal Ahold price, compared to that of Carrefour and Walmart
Source: G. Maertens, Datastream (2014).

the board were in the board of other companies. There were directors who weren't really independent. For example, several directors were managers or ex-managers of the company. R.J. Nelissen was also member of the board of directors of the auditor, and Sir Perry worked at Unilever, an important supplier of Royal Ahold. There were also directors who came from politics, but weren't qualified, like C.P. Schneider, an art teacher and former US ambassador to the Netherlands who, in June 2003, in the middle of the storm, admitted she didn't have business training and wasn't qualified to understand the accounts.

The company's CEO (Cees van der Hoeven), the CFO (Michiel Meurs), the president of the Supervision Committee (Henny de Ruiter), the president of the American subsidiary, and other executives resigned or were dismissed.

Dutch authorities imposed on Royal Ahold an 8-million-euro fine. The CEO, the manager responsible for Europe, the marketing director, and two purchasing managers were convicted. Everyone had to pay monetary sanctions and some were sentenced to prison, that in some cases reached up to four years.

Since the company also traded on Wall Street, the American SEC fined Royal Ahold with $11 million. Executives from companies supplying Royal Ahold, like Tyson Foods and General Mills, were also convicted.

Comments on the Case

This case shows several problems of motivation and opportunity, such as:

Motivation Problems

A very aggressive remuneration system that rewarded growth instead of the creation of value for shareholders.

Listed company.

Very ambitious growth objectives that weren't being achieved.

Opportunity Problems

Lack of independence, preparation, and dedication of a good part of the board of directors.

Predominance of managers and directors appointed by the CEO.

(Continued)

The chief executive officer (CEO) was also chief financial officer (CFO).

Ex-employees and former managers on the board.

Key Topics of the Chapter:

- The Triangle of Fraud considers three factors that lead to committing fraud:
  1. Motivation: The need or pressure that encourages the interest in defrauding.
  2. Opportunity: A situation that allows defrauding with a low risk level. The existence of opportunities makes it easier for frauds to occur.
  3. Rationalization: The mental frame that justifies a person committing fraud.

The door to fraud includes a fourth element, the fraudster's profile:

- Ability: The skills of the fraudster without which the fraud could not be committed.

- Arrogance: It explains why some people have unlimited greed and the feeling of impunity by believing that company rules don't affect them.

- Intentions of the fraudster: Depending on the intention we can differentiate between an accidental fraud committed by someone who didn't necessarily have the intention to do it and the fraud committed by a predator.

REFERENCES

Abarnell, J., and Lehavy, R. (2003). Can Stock Recommendations Predict Earnings Management and Analysts? *Journal of Accounting Research* (March).

Ahold (2003). Anual Report 2002.

Baker, C.R, Cohanier, B., and Leo, N.J. (2016). Considerations beyond the fraud triangle in the fraud at Société Générale, *Journal of Forensic & Investigative Accounting* 8 (3, July–December).

Beasley, M.S. (1996): An empirical analysis of the relation between the board of director composition and financial statement fraud. *The Accounting Review* 71(4): 443–465.

Cressey, D. (1980). *Encyclopedia of Criminological Theory*. SAGE Publications Inc.

Cressey, D.R. (1986). Why managers commit fraud. Australian and New Zealand. *Journal of Criminology.* 19 (4): 195–209.

Gil de Albornoz, B., and Illueca, M. (2003). Regulación de precios y prácticas de *earnings management:* Evidencia empírica en el sector eléctrico español, *Revista de contabilidad y Tributación* 247: 443–463.

Kranacher, M.J., Riley, R., and Wells, J. (2010). *Forensic Accounting and Fraud Examination.* : Hoboken, NJ: Wiley.

Marks, J. (2010). *Playing Offense in a High-Risk Environment.* New York: Crowe Horwath International, LLC.

McLean, B. (2001). Why Enron went bust start with arrogance. Add greed, deceit, and financial chicanery. What do you get? A company that wasn't what it was cracked up to be. *Fortune Magazine* 24 (December).

Mock, J.M. (2004). *Classic Case Studies in Accounting Fraud.* Thesis, Miami University. https://etd.ohiolink.edu/!etd.send_file%3Faccession%3Dmzuhonors1111 004894%26disposition%3Dinline.

Wolfe, D.T., and Hermanson, D.R. (2004). The fraud diamond: Considering the four elements of fraud. *The CPA Journal.* December.

Zayas, L. (2016). Señales de alerta para la detección de fraude en las empresas. *Revista de Contabilidad y Dirección* 23.

CHAPTER 5

Legal Accounting Manipulations

*The loopholes and the flexibility of the accounting standards allow
for a wide variety of financial results.*

—James A. Largay (about the lessons from the Enron case)

5.1 ALTERNATIVES, ESTIMATIONS, AND LEGAL GAPS

We have previously talked about legal accounting manipulation. It is a posting that, although it doesn't infringe the accounting standards, is done so the accounts show the image that those who prepare the accounts are interested in, instead of being done objectively. In some cases it can be a fraud of law, since, although the rules are being applied, there are practices that pursue goals that are against what is intended by the accounting standards.

If there are legal manipulations it is, basically, due to the regulations' flexibility. This explains why some companies manipulate their accounts relying on the accounting standards. It is an international problem because no country escapes from the excessive flexibility of the accounting standards.

A study published by *CFO* magazine in 1998 established that 78% of financial directors stated having received instructions to use the accounting standards to get the accounts to offer a better image; 38% admitted following these instructions.

Next, we review the main aspects that make the accounting standards have a wide margin of flexibility.

Transactions That Can Be Accounted for by Choosing Among Several Alternatives

In the accounting standards there are many transactions that can be reflected in the accounting using different alternatives. This enables using more prudent or more aggressive accounting alternatives according to the interest.

47

THE METRO TRAINS

Amador (2012) analyzes the following case, referred to as the 2008 accounts of *Metro de Madrid*. These accounts reported that several trains, financed with 17-year leases, had been put into operation. These contracts implied installments payable for the amount of 6,375 million euros. Given that the term of the contract coincided with the trains' useful life it seems clear that it had to be reflected as a financial leasing and, therefore, it was necessary to activate the trains and reflect the debt in the liabilities.

However, the company relied in an opinion requested from a law firm that endorsed the thesis that it was an operative lease because, in their opinion, the risks and benefits of the trains hadn't been transferred to *Metro de Madrid*. Based on this opinion, the company didn't activate the trains nor did it include the financing received in the liabilities, which allowed the companies to reflect a lower level of debt. In any case, the company was informed about this issue in the report.

It is a questionable practice, but it could possibly be argued that it didn't go against the law.

The current formulation of some of the accounting principles greatly favors the level of flexibility. In this sense, we can recall the content of the principles of uniformity and of relative importance.

Uniformity

There are cases in which companies change the accounting criteria used from one year to another. Although it is mandatory to use the accounting criteria uniformly throughout the years, what is usually done in case of change of criteria is to explain in the report that the circumstances that had once motivated the use of a certain criterion have changed. Moreover, the change of accounting criterion must be informed by the auditor in his report which has to present the change as an exception.

Relative Importance

According to this principle, nonstrict application of some accounting principles and criteria is allowed when the relative importance, in quantitative and/or qualitative terms, of the variation that this occurrence produces is scarcely significant and, as a consequence, doesn't alter the expression of true image. The problem is that the accounting standards don't include a guideline that allows quantifying when a topic is important or not. This can lead to different interpretations.

On the other hand, there are moments in which regulators authorize especial treatments that enable the accounts to show a better image. For example in 2008, due to the aggressiveness of the global financial crisis, several countries authorized not posting losses due to the impairment of real estate. This allowed many companies that had been seriously affected by the impairment of their real estate not to go into bankruptcy.

Accounting Notes Based on Estimates That Imply a High Degree of Subjectivity

There are many transactions that, to be accounted for, require subjective estimates, more or less optimistic, about future events. This affects, for example, the quantification of the impairment (loss of value of assets) and the provisions (pensions, severance pay, etc.).

An example of an interesting estimation is to calculate the impairment due to a customers' defaulting with optimistic (or pessimistic) criteria to increase (or reduce) profits. Another example is the criterion used to estimate indirect production expenses, which are incorporated into the products in progress and finished.

There are times when an external professional is employed to make the estimates. For example, for pensions, an actuary can be hired to set the future contingencies. In this case, the valuation can be manipulated by choosing a known appraiser to do a pessimistic or optimistic assessment, taking into account that the valuation of the pension debt depends on the estimates made on:

- Staff's mortality and life expectancy tables
- Foreseeable evolution of the current workforce with right to pension
- Employee turnover
- Foreseeable evolution of salaries, contribution bases, and Social Security benefits
- Evolution of the structure of the current staff, regarding seniority, category, position, and so forth
- Retirement age

And we must also consider factors such as:

- Expected rates for future inflation
- Increases in pension
- Death of employees before retirement
- Profitability of investments in which the resources of the pensions plan materialize

If accounting is based on estimates, rather than facts, the possibility of accounting manipulations increases. To get an idea of the importance of this topic, we have analyzed the number of times the word *estimate*, or a derivation of the same term, appears in the annual accounts of the companies included in the European stock index EUROSTOXX for the year 2016 and in most companies it appears between 15 and 110 times. The estimates affect the majority of the most relevant items of the annual accounts.

Also, the problem of estimates worsens every day, since companies are increasingly using estimates in the formulation of their accounts. According to Lev (2016), the average of estimates that a company of the S&P 500 index makes has gone from 30 in 1995 to 148 in 2013.

Gaps in the Accounting Standards

There are also new transactions for which there are gaps in the regulation.

An example is the so-called *nonrecourse debt*: There are companies, usually big builders, that project finance through nonrecourse debt. For this, the most common way is using a subsidiary that only has the assets and liabilities of the project. In this type of operation, the bank's guarantee is given by the group that creates the subsidiary but only until the project is completed. Once the construction is completed, the only guarantee becomes the subsidiary that has received the loan, so the guarantee is the asset that has been built. For example, if a nuclear plant is built and it is financed with nonrecourse debt, in case of default in the repayment of the loan, the guarantee is:

- In the construction phase, the guarantee is the group that creates the subsidiary.
- Once the construction of the plant is completed, the guarantee becomes the subsidiary and, therefore, the plant itself, which is what it has in its assets.

On the other hand, if it was a recourse debt, in a case of nonpayment, the lender could keep the nuclear plant, but could also demand payment from the subsidiary group that received the loan. There are companies that, taking advantage of the accounting standards' lack of concretization on the treatment of nonrecourse debt, do not include the nonrecourse debt in the liabilities. In other cases, the debt is done with a contract that is difficult to understand, in which it isn't clear whether the borrower has to answer for the debt in case of default and takes advantage of this circumstance to not reflect the debt as a liability of the borrower.

These manipulations are used to reduce the debt.

THE LEGAL VOID LEHMAN BROTHERS TOOK ADVANTAGE OF

As mentioned in previous chapters, in 2008 this entity went bankrupt after a 50-million-dollar accounting scandal became known.

Despite the fraud committed, the court didn't declare them guilty because it wasn't proven that any rule had been violated. Lehman Brothers had taken advantage of gaps in the accounting standards to manipulate the accounts. The accounting manipulations consisted in selling failed loans to its subsidiaries in the Cayman Islands with the agreement to repurchase them later. This way, it offered the image of having $50 million in treasury, instead of worthless loans. Therefore, it was hiding multimillion-dollar losses. However, the subsidiaries' nonconsolidation of accounts allowed Lehman Brothers to present accounts without these failed loans.

A year earlier, in 2007, the prestigious magazine *Fortune* named Lehman Brothers "The most admired investment company."

In her statement on April 20th, 2010, before the US Congress, Mary L. Schapiro (president of the US Securities and Exchange Commission (SEC)) declared that Lehman's bankruptcy had many causes, and among them, several related to bad regulation and legal gaps.

- Irresponsible concession of loans, that were facilitated by a securitization process that was initially seen as a risk reduction mechanism.
- Proliferation of derivatives and other complex financial instruments, that weren't transparent and weren't comprehensible for most of those who invested in them or were financed by them. The accounting practices didn't reflect adequately the debts and risks these products presented.
- Perverse incentive systems that encouraged managers to take excessive risks.
- Insufficient risk control by the companies involved in the commercialization and purchase of complex financial instruments.
- Excessive reliance on rating agencies' assessment.
- A deregulation that gave way to weaker rules and normative gaps.
- Investment banks' regulation and supervision mistakes, who only detected the problem when it was already too late.

(Continued)

On Lehman Brothers, Bruce Dubinsky, from the Association of Fraud Examiners, stated in 2013: "Lehman & Brothers ... took advantage of a gap in the accounting standards to hide losses in their financial statements ... Hopefully managers, auditors and regulators have learned the lesson."

5.2 MAIN LEGAL MANIPULATIONS

Below are the main types of legal accounting manipulations that some companies practice to:

- Increase or reduce assets (see Figure 5.1).
- Increase or reduce debts (see Figure 5.2).

	Increases in Assets	**Reduction in Assets**
Tangible Fixed Assets	■ Optimistic estimates on the useful life, annual wear, costs of dismantling, etc. ■ Apply the revalued value (when the regulation allows it) instead of the historical cost. ■ Reverse impairments from previous years. ■ Activate expenses (financial, exchange differences, etc.). ■ Valuate higher assets in a merger. ■ Increase the work done for fixed assets. ■ Post leasing as financial leases. ■ Method for obtaining a higher fair value (active market price, average of recent transactions, cash flows discount, etc.) ■ Method to obtain a higher value of the value in use. ■ Depreciate less.	■ Pessimistic estimates on the useful life, annual wear, costs of dismantling, etc. ■ Apply the historical cost instead of revaluing (although the regulation allows revaluation). ■ Not activate expenses (financial, exchange differences, etc.). ■ Valuate lower assets in a merger. ■ Reduce the work done for fixed assets. ■ Post leasing as operating leases ■ Method for obtaining a lower fair value (active market price, average of recent transactions, cash flows discount, etc.) ■ Method to obtain a lower value of the value in use. ■ Depreciate more.
Intangible Fixed Assets	■ Optimistic estimates on concessions: future flows, discount rate, etc. ■ Activate expenses (research and development, computer programs developed within the company, repairs, maintenance, advertising, etc.)	■ Pessimistic estimates on concessions: future flows, discount rate, etc. ■ Not activate expenses (research and development, computer programs developed within the company, repairs, maintenance, advertising, etc.).

FIGURE 5.1 Accounting manipulations (that are possibly) legal to increase or reduce assets

	Increases in Assets	Reduction in Assets
	▪ Impute more indirect expenses to projects. ▪ Deteriorate less the Goodwill with optimistic estimates. ▪ Amortize less.	▪ Impute less indirect expenses to projects ▪ Deteriorate more the Goodwill with pessimistic estimates. ▪ Amortize more.
Financial Fixed Assets	▪ Use lower interest rates to increase the current value of future charges. ▪ Use the consolidation method that increases more the value. ▪ Method to obtain a higher value of the current value of the financial asset, discount rate used. ▪ Consideration of the instrument as a trading portfolio or as available for sale, depending on which offers a higher value.	▪ Use higher interest rates to reduce the current value of future charges. ▪ Use the consolidation method that reduces more the value. ▪ Method to obtain a lower value of the current value of the financial asset, discount rate used. ▪ Consideration of the instrument as a trading portfolio or as available for sale, depending on which offers a lower value
Deferred Tax Assets	▪ Activate corporate tax when there are losses, assuming they may be compensated for in the future.	▪ Not activate corporate tax when there are losses, assuming they can't be compensated for in the future.
Inventory	▪ Optimistic estimates about the impairment. ▪ Change the inventory assessment criterion (first in, first out, average). ▪ Quantification of the production cost by allocating more indirect manufacturing costs. ▪ Choose between the percentage of completion method and the completed contract method, depending on which gives a higher inventory value.	▪ Pessimistic estimates about the impairment. ▪ Change the inventory assessment criterion (first in, first out, average). ▪ Quantification of the production cost by allocating less Indirect manufacturing costs. ▪ Choose between the percentage of completion method and the completed contract method, depending on which gives a lower inventory value.
Customers	▪ Optimistic estimates on payment default. ▪ Optimistic estimate of the current value when the cash flow occurs within more than one year	▪ Pessimistic estimates on payment default. ▪ Finance customer balances with nonrecourse factoring, thereby eliminating the customer balances from the assets. ▪ Pessimistic estimate of the current value when the cash flow occurs within more than one year.

FIGURE 5.1 (*Continued*)

- Reclassify assets or debts to change the structure of the assets and/or the debts (see Figure 5.3).
- Increase or reduce profits (see Figure 5.4).

	Increases in Debt	Reductions in Debt
Financial Liabilities	■ Use lower interest rates to increase current value of future payments ■ Post leasing as financial leases ■ Consideration of the debt (factoring or similar) as recourse debt and thus include it in the balance sheet. ■ Consolidate by the global integration method to integrate the total debt of the subsidiaries.	■ Consideration of debt (factoring or similar) as nonrecourse. ■ Get into debt through unconsolidated subsidiaries. ■ Use higher interest rates to reduce the current value of future payments. ■ Post leasing as operating leases. ■ Consideration of the debt (factoring or similar) as nonrecourse debt and thus remove it from the balance sheet (it remains as off-balance financing). ■ Consolidate by the partial integration method or by the participation method to integrate less debt of the subsidiaries.
Provisions (dismantling of assets, lawsuits, prosecutions, liabilities, pensions)	■ Pessimistic estimates. ■ Consolidate by the global integration method to integrate the total provisions of the subsidiaries.	■ Optimistic estimates. ■ Consolidate by the partial integration method or by the participation method to integrate less provisions of the subsidiaries.
Suppliers	■ Pessimistic estimates of the current value when the cash flow is produced within more than a year. Consolidate by the global integration method to integrate the total debt of the subsidiaries.	■ Get in debt through unconsolidated subsidiaries. ■ Pessimistic estimates of the current value when the cash flow is produced within more than a year. ■ Consolidate by the partial integration method or by the participation method to integrate less debt of the subsidiaries.

FIGURE 5.2 Accounting manipulations (that are possibly) legal to increase or reduce debts

	Increases in Assets	Reductions in Assets
Non-Current Assets	■ Include long-cycle inventory in the non-current assets (for example, wine-making companies). ■ Revert the consideration of property in current assets by classifying them as non-current assets held for sale.	■ Include property in current assets by classifying them as non-current assets held for sale.
Non-Current Assets Kept for Sale	■ Include property in current assets by classifying them as non-current assets held for sale.	■ Reverse the property consideration in current asset by classifying them as non-current assets held for sale.
Inventory	■ Include long-cycle inventory in inventory (for example, in wine-making companies). ■ Add advances to suppliers to inventory.	■ Include long-cycle inventory in non-current assets (for example, wine-making companies). ■ Subtract advances from suppliers from the suppliers account.
Temporary Financial Investments	■ Not considering financial instruments as high-liquidity investments, to classify them as treasury rather than temporary financial investments.	■ Consideration of financial instruments as high-liquidity investments, to classify them as treasury, rather than temporary financial investments.
Treasury	■ Consideration of financial instruments as high-liquidity investments, to classify them as treasury, rather than temporary financial investments.	■ Not considering financial instruments as high-liquidity investments, to classify them as treasury rather than temporary financial investments.

FIGURE 5.3 Account categories (that are possibly) legal to reclassify asset items

The reclassification of items, although it seems it shouldn't alter the image offered by a company, in some cases may have relevant impact. For example, placing an advance payment to a supplier as less current liabilities or as a current asset can change the liquidity ratio (current assets/current liabilities).

Reclassifications are also used to manipulate cash flow statements when flows from operations are reflected as if they were from financing or investment (or vice versa). It is also possible to manipulate in the income statement by reclassifying operating items as if they were exceptional or from discontinued operations (or vice versa).

	Increases in Profit	Reductions in Profit
Income	■ Anticipate income recognition. ■ Anticipate income in long-term contracts using the percentage of completion method. ■ Anticipate income in operations carried out over several fiscal years. ■ Optimistic estimates on sales returns. ■ Increase work done for fixed assets. Consider as income the interests incorporated into the credits for sales, with maturity not exceeding 12 months.	■ Defer income recognition. ■ Defer income in long-term contracts by using the completed contract method. ■ Delay income in operations carried out over several fiscal years. ■ Pessimistic estimates on sales returns. ■ Reduce work done for fixed assets. ■ Not include the interests incorporated into the credits with maturity not exceeding 12 months.
Research and Development Expense	■ Activate the research and development expense.	■ Not activating the research and development expense.
Depreci-ations	■ Optimistic estimates on useful life and depreciation of non-current assets. ■ Delay the start of the depreciation of an asset (when the asset is in operating conditions).	■ Pessimistic estimates on useful life and depreciation of non-current assets. ■ Advance the start of the depreciation of an asset (when the asset is in operating conditions).
Other Expenses	■ Activate expenses (repairs, maintenance, advertising, etc.). ■ Defer acknowledgement of expenses. ■ Imputation of negative conversion differences of foreign subsidiaries to the equity.	■ Not activate expenses (repairs, maintenance, advertising, etc.) ■ Anticipate the acknowledgment of expenses ■ Imputation of negative conversion differences of foreign subsidiaries to the result.
Other Income	■ Imputation of positive conversion differences of foreign subsidiaries to the result.	■ Imputation of positive conversion differences of foreign subsidiaries to the equity.
Provisions	■ Optimistic estimates on provisions (pension plans, restructuring, taxes, pending trials in court, etc.). ■ Consider a provision unnecessary.	■ Pessimistic estimates on provisions (pension plans, restructuring, taxes, pending trials in court, etc.) ■ Consider a provision necessary.

FIGURE 5.4 Accounting manipulations (that are possibly) legal to increase or reduce profits

	Increases in Profit	**Reductions in Profit**
Impairment of Assets	■ Optimistic estimates on the value of assets. ■ Deteriorate less the optimistic estimates for good will. ■ Consideration of financial instruments as available for sale to allocate their loss of value losses in the equity, instead of in a trading portfolio (which should go in the income statement).	■ Consideration of financial instruments as available for sale to allocate their increases in value in equity, Instead of as trading portfolio (which should go in the income statement). ■ Pessimistic estimates of the value of assets. ■ Deteriorate more the pessimistic estimates for good will.
Exceptional Results	■ Sell non-current assets generating positive results.	■ Sell non-current assets generating negative results.
Financial Expenses and Income	■ Activate financial expenses. ■ Activate exchange differences. ■ Incorporate as income the interests of credits with maturity not exceeding 12 months.	■ Not activate financial expenses. ■ Not activate exchange differences. ■ Not incorporating as income the interests of credits with maturity not exceeding 12 months.
Corporate Tax	■ Activate the corporate tax when there are losses, assuming in can be compensated for in the future.	■ Not activate the corporate tax when there are losses, assuming in can't be compensated for in the future.

FIGURE 5.4 (*Continued*)

MANIPULATING THE OPERATING RESULT IN A COMMERCIAL COMPANY

This company had significant losses due to the accelerated expansion in its number of stores. From year 3 it started to close the stores with deficits, and reflected it in the income statement as an extraordinary item. This way, it was able to offer an operating result that grew steadily.

At press conferences it only reported the operating result, which explains that the media didn't highlight that the company was actually generating losses.

	Year 1	Year 2	Year 3	Year 4
Operating result	+58	+63	+66	+74
Exceptional income and expenses	−2	−6	−71	−96
Earnings before tax	+56	+57	−5	−22

COOKING THE RESULT AT TRUMP HOTELS & CASINOS RESORTS

According to *Fortune* (2016), in 2002, Donald J. Trump's casino empire in Atlantic City was accused of fraudulent information by the SEC.

	1998	1999	Growth
Income	397	403	+1.5%
Net result	5	14	+180%

The 1999 result didn't include an extraordinary expense of $81 million to update the old-fashioned Trump World's Fair Hotel & Casino. On the other hand, it did include the extraordinary profit of $17 million for the cancelling of a lease of the All Star Café in the Taj Mahal Casino. According to the SEC, the result of 1999 should have been negative. When the company adjusted the results following the instructions of the SEC, the share price went down. A few years later, in 2005, the company went bankrupt.

5.3   IMPACT OF LEGAL MANIPULATIONS IN THE ACCOUNTS

The impact of legal accounting manipulations can be highly relevant. As an example, Figure 5.5 shows the result of applying to a real company the most conservative and less conservative criteria included in the IFRS and US GAAP. The company's result, with the most common criteria of the IFRS, has been put on base 100. It can be seen that the result of this company, according to the IFRS, can fluctuate between −46 and +140. As an example, when accounting for the research and development expense, it has been posted as an expense in More Conservative Criteria and as assets in Less Conservative Criteria, taking into account that both methods are accepted by the accounting regulation.

This example shows that the IFRS regulation is the one that offers higher flexibility. These data are consistent with several studies (for example, Callao and Jarne, 2010) that show that the IFRS offer more possibilities of alternative treatment and estimates compared to other accounting standards.

Rules Applied to a Company's Transactions	Most Common Criteria	More Conservative Criteria	Less Conservative Criteria
International Financial Reporting Standards	100	–46	140
US GAAP	76	66	106

FIGURE 5.5 Alterations in the profits of a company using different accounting standards
Source: Author's own work. The most common, the more conservative, and the less conservative accounting criteria have been applied to the transactions of a company done in 2014. The company's profit is put on base 100 according to the most common accounting criteria included in IFRS.

A study by the ACCID (2017) concludes that in the IFRS there are over one hundred transactions that allow alternative accounting treatment and subjective estimates.

Key Topics of the Chapter

- Legal accounting manipulation consists of making a posting that, although it doesn't infringe the accounting rules, is done so the accounts show the image that interests to those who prepare the accounts, instead of being done objectively.
- Legal accounting manipulation is a consequence of the rules' flexibility and is usually done through three types of transactions:
  1. Transactions that can be accounted for choosing among several alternatives.
  2. Accounting notes based on more or less optimistic estimates.
  3. Gaps in accounting regulations.
- In the accounting standards there are multiple transactions that may be object of alternative accounting treatments or that require the use of subjective estimates to be accounted for.
- Legal accounting manipulations can affect significantly all the items of the accounts: assets, liabilities, income, expenses and results.

REFERENCES

ACCID. (2008). *El Nuevo PGC y el PGC pymes*. Barcelona: ACCID-Profit.
ACCID. (2017). *Comprender las Normas Internacionales de Contabilidad*. Barcelona: ACCID.

Amador, S. (2012). Contabilidad creativa. *Contabilidad y Tributación 347*.

Callao, S. and Jarne, J.I. (2010). Have IFRS affected earnings management in the European Union? *Accounting in Europe* 7 (1): 159–188.

Fortune (2016). *When Donald Trump Got in Trouble with the SEC.* http://fortune .com/2016/03/14/donald-trump-sec/.

Largay, J. (2002). Lessons from Enron. *Accounting Horizons* 16 (2): 154.

Mohrle, S.R. (2002). Do firms use restructuring charge reversals to meet earnings targets? *The Accounting Review* 77 (2): 397–423.

Penman, S.H. and Zhang, X. (2002). Accounting conservatism, the quality of earnings, and stock returns. *The Accounting Review* 77 (2): 237–264.

CHAPTER 6

CHAPTER 6

Illegal Accounting Manipulations

The world's leading company.

—Plaque in the lobby of Enron's headquarters

6.1 ACCOUNTING CRIME

Illegal accounting manipulation is a practice that isn't allowed by legislation. It is an accounting crime since it implies falseness in the accounting documents. In most countries, accounting crime is punished with prison. In this case, falseness is understood as the omission of information or the provision of fictitious information. Falseness is considered a crime when it prevents knowing the true financial situation of the company and, also, causes a loss. And, there must be fraud, meaning, an awareness that the law is being infringed and the intention to cause damage harming a third party. Those responsible for the crime are the authors and their accomplices.

Illegal accounting manipulation is usually done by keeping different accountings, also known as double accounting, where one is used on tax declarations, and the other one allows us to know the company's real situation. When illegal manipulations are discovered, there can be fines or even prison sentences. These rulings affect those responsible for the crime, who usually are the businessman and the accountant (when acting as an accomplice to the businessman).

THE CASE OF THE COMPANY THAT KEPT A TRIPLE ACCOUNTING

It was a company that kept an official accounting that was the one used for tax declaration and the deposit of accounts in the Mercantile Registry. Also, it kept an accounting called *private* that was used

(Continued)

---

to inform shareholders. This accounting reflected higher profits than those declared to the tax office, but lower than the reality since the majority shareholder wanted to hide a part of the profits from the other shareholders to avoid paying excessive dividends.

Finally, it kept the third accounting, called *super private*, that reflected the reality of the profits generated by the company.

The most curious thing about this case is that the majority shareholder hid the reality from the other shareholders, who were his own brothers, since they didn't work in the company and were always asking for more dividends.

Let's see an example of illegal accounting manipulation,

INCOME SMOOTHING WITH UNREAL LOSSES AT FREDDIE MAC

In 2003, the Securities and Exchange Commission (SEC) discovered that Freddie Mac, the second biggest financial entity in the United States in the mortgage loans sector, had reduced its profits by $5 million between 2000 and 2002. The fraud was carried out through derivative financial instruments through which it reflected unrealistic losses. It was also done by deteriorating credits with a higher delinquency than it actually had. The goal of the manipulation was to meet the profit forecasts done by analysts and to pay fewer taxes in some years. Figure 6.1 shows that what the company did was income smoothing, reducing the profits in 2000 to increase them in 2001. It can be verified that with the smoothing the profits increased each year, when in reality they reduced in 2001.

Year	Declared Earnings	Adjusted Earnings after the Scandal	Difference
2000	2,547	3,666	+1,119
2001	4,147	3,158	−989
2002	5,764	10,090	+4,326

FIGURE 6.1 Declared earnings, adjusted earnings, and difference (manipulation done) in Freddie Mac from 2000 to 2002. Data in millions of dollars
Source: Author's own work from the accounts of the company.

President David Glenn, CEO Lelan Bredsel, CFO Vaughn Clarke, and Vice-President Nazir Dossani were fired and fined $400,000 each. The company also paid a fine of $125 million, besides several financial sanctions.

A year later, it was discovered that Fannie Mae (the main competitor of Freddie Mac) had done the same type of fraud.

6.2 HOW ILLEGAL MANIPULATIONS ARE DONE

In the International Standards on Auditing (ISA 240) the following practices are considered accounting frauds:

- Manipulation, falsification, or alteration of accounting records
- Misrepresentation or intentional omission of facts or other meaningful information in the financial statements
- Intentional misapplication of accounting principles

Accounting fraud is done by:

- Increasing or reducing assets (conceal assets, incorporate nonexistent assets, use unreal acquisition prices, etc.).
- Increasing or reducing debts (concealing debts, incorporate nonexistent debts, inflate debts, etc.).
- Increasing or reducing profits (hide or inflate profits unrealistically, use prices far from the market price, anticipate income, conceal of inflate expenses, or post them as reserves without going through the income statement; depreciations, provisions and illegal impairments, etc.). The posting of fictitious sales is one of the most widespread accounting frauds and, in addition to the cases shown in this book, there are other famous scandals in which this type of fraud was performed (Durex, a manufacturer of condoms, increased its profits by 90 million pounds in the year 2000 with fictitious sales).

Invented Assets in Colonial Bank and TBW

In August 2009, two American companies went bankrupt, Taylor, Bean & Whitaker (TBW, which specialized in granting mortgages) and Colonial Bank.

(Continued)

The cause of these bankruptcies was a fraud that began seven years earlier and consisted of TBW selling to Colonial Bank mortgages that were actually junk mortgages, in some cases, and in others cases they were nonexistent mortgages. This fraud generated a total loss of $6.5 million to clients, depositors, employees, and the government. Of this loss, $4.2 million had to be paid by a government fund, the Federal Deposit Insurance Corp.

TBW was a company characterized by an excess of luxury (a private jet, a seaplane, antique car collections, etc.).

The scandal became public when Colonial Bank had no cash to return deposits to its clients.

Soon after the scandal the trials were held and Lee Farkas (former president of TBW) was convicted to 30 years in prison. Cathy Kissick (former vice-president of Colonial Back) and Paul Allen (former CEO of TWB) were sentenced in 2011 to eight years and five years in prison, respectively.

The Fraud of James Whitaker Wright with Fictitious Operations Between Unconsolidated Companies

James Whitaker Wright was born in Surrey, England, in 1846. In 1890 he created the London and Globe Company that invested in silver mines and was the head of the Wright Group. It was a highly respected group because both its president and the majority of the members of the board of directors were aristocrats. James Whitaker, who lived with great luxuries and rubbed shoulders with British royalty, selected aristocrats for senior positions in his company in order to impress investors and customers.

Later, James Whitaker wanted to be valued as a businessman who cared about his city. Thus, he emitted bonds to finance the Bakerloo line of the London Underground. However, the emission was a disaster and he didn't get investors. Instead of acknowledging it, he wanted to hide it using funds from his business group. This caused the loss of capital of the Wright Group. When the group started to get in trouble, he hid it with a series of fictitious sales between companies of the group that didn't consolidate, which made it impossible to see that things weren't going well. However, at the end of 1900 James Whitaker announced his companies wouldn't pay dividends. This fact caused investor's distrust since it wasn't logical to suspend dividends when the accounts of the Wright Group gave the image that everything was going well. Immediately, the group went bankrupt. James Whitaker tried to run, but he was found and taken to trial.

When, in 1904, the judge sentenced him to seven years in prison, at the headquarters of London's Royal Court of Justice, he swallowed a cyanide tablet and died instantly.

6.3 OPERATIONS THROUGH TAX HAVENS

Operations through tax havens don't have to be illegal. However, it should be remembered that, according to the Organisation for Economic Co-operation and Development (OECD), tax havens are distinguished by:

- Low taxation.
- Lack of transparency due to fewer disclosure requirements.
- The exchange of information with other countries for tax reasons isn't allowed.
- Nonresidents are allowed to benefit from tax reductions even when they don't actually carry out an activity in the country.

The combination of these four requirements explains that most of the accounting scandals that occurred in the last decades were done through subsidiaries in tax havens (Enron, Parmalat, etc.).

Tax havens are small countries (Cayman Islands, Jersey Island, Gibraltar, for example) where hundreds of thousands of companies that are subsidiaries of companies of other countries are domiciled.

In many cases the operations don't violate the law and are simply tax avoidance practices (in principle, legal operations to reduce taxation), which is different from tax evasion (illegally hiding goods or income to pay less tax). In 2016, Christian Kem, president of Austria, reported these practices reminding that:

Every sausage stand pays more tax in Austria than a multinational corporation. That goes for Starbucks, Amazon and other companies.

In fact, in 2014, according to Christian Kem, Starbucks paid in Austria 1,400 euros in corporate tax. Surely these companies perform legal practices, though it is more debatable whether or not these practices are ethical.

Something similar occurs with several multinationals of information and communication technologies (ICT) like Apple, Microsoft, Yahoo, Facebook, eBay, and Amazon. They have their headquarters is in the United States and subsidiaries in several European countries, but their European headquarters are usually located in Ireland. In this country's subsidiary is where most of the profits generated in the rest of European subsidiaries accumulate. For this, the subsidiaries of countries with higher taxes become mere commission agents, since the activities developed in Europe are invoiced from Ireland.

Another option is for the subsidiaries of higher taxing countries to buy the products from the Irish subsidiary at a high price, allowing profits to concentrate in Ireland. This explains why many of these multinationals register losses or few profits in European countries. Google, for example, declares losses in many European subsidiaries, which in fact are sales forces that only invoice expenses to the Irish branch, which is the one that makes the profits in Europe. Similarly, Starbucks has registered losses in the UK in 14 of the past 15 years, as a consequence of the high royalties it pays to its subsidiaries in the Netherlands and Switzerland.

Ireland's appeal is that it has a 12.5% income tax rate, while in other counties this percentage is much higher and is between 20% and 30%. In addition, many multinationals use companies in the Netherlands that don't have employees and allow them to end up taxing just over 1% of the profits produced in Europe. This type of Dutch company is called a front company, because from there the money is sent to tax havens.

One question that arises is, at what point is it a legal practice? In principle, although tax havens and other strategies are used to reduce to the minimum the fiscal invoices, these are legal activities. In fact, what they do is pay the minimum taxes, taking advantage of the different tax regulations in each country, which is logical in companies where the main goal is to maximize the profits it generates for shareholders.

Therefore, we aren't talking about an underground economy or violating the current legislation. However, maybe it could be a fraud of law, because it obeys the law but to obtain results contrary to those pursued by the regulations. There are also complaints about the unfair competition that produces the reduction of the fiscal invoice in relation to companies that do comply with it.

Another topic is the ethical dimension. In 2014 the British Parliament concluded it is a reprehensible immorality. This can affect the company's reputation, so that it is not a surprise that Starbucks, for example, has announced that from now on it will pay more taxes in Europe.

In spite of the above, the fact that the big accounting scandals have been done through subsidiaries in tax havens leads us to intuit that tax havens are a sign to pay attention to. Thus, for example, Portillo and Morales (2015) explain that the most commonly used methods to carry out tax frauds are fake invoices and transactions through companies located in tax havens.

Many accounting frauds have been done through what is called triangular operations.

Triangular Operation

Company A is interested in reducing profits to pay less corporate tax.

Let's imagine it purchases goods for 2 euros and resells it to company B for 20 euros. In this case, the profit amounts to 18 euros.

The triangular operation could consist of using a company C (a subsidiary in a tax haven). This company would acquire the goods for 2 euros and would sell it to company A for 19.9 euros.

Later, company A resells the goods for 20 euros to company B. In this case, company A's profit has been reduced to 0.1 euros, since most of the benefit is obtained by company C (17.9 euros), which by being located in a tax haven can enjoy low or zero taxation.

The Paradisiacal Island of Sark

Sark is a small island in the English Channel that has an extension of 5.4 square kilometers and a population of about 600 people. It has very low taxation since there is no income tax, nor capital gains tax, nor inheritance tax. In 1565, Queen Elizabeth I granted the title of Lord of the island to the nobleman Hellier de Carteret and the command of the island in compensation for the defense against pirate attacks. In payment for this privilege, the Lord had to pay each year 1.79 pounds to the British Crown. This feudal regime lasted until 2008, a year in which the first democratic elections were celebrated. Given the orography of the island, cars aren't allowed and only tractors can circulate on the road.

We tell this whole story because, according to King (1998), over 100,000 companies have subsidiaries in the island of Sark. From the above, we can ask ourselves:

What are over a 100,000 companies doing in the Island of Sark?

Is what they do is legal? Is what they do is ethical?

6.4 MAIN ILLEGAL MANIPULATIONS

The following figures show the main types of accounting manipulations that can be done. They are manipulations done to:

- Increase or reduce assets (see Figure 6.2).
- Increase or reduce debts (see Figure 6.3).
- Increase or reduce profits (see Figure 6.4).

	Increases of Assets	Reductions of Assets
Noncurrent Assets	▪ Incorporate inexistent assets (work in progress, goodwill, etc.) ▪ Activate expenses fraudulently ▪ Increase fictitiously the value of noncurrent assets ▪ Amortize (or make provisions or deteriorate) noncurrent assets less than prescribed by the regulation ▪ Excess deferred tax assets in a company with many losses	▪ Hide noncurrent assets ▪ Reduce fictitiously the value of noncurrent assets ▪ Amortize (or make provisions or deteriorate) noncurrent assets more than prescribed by the regulation
Financial Investments	▪ Inventing financial investments ▪ Mark down financial investments less than prescribed by the regulation ▪ Use of difficult-to-understand derivative financial instruments to hide fraud	▪ Hide financial investments ▪ Mark up financial investments prescribed by the regulation ▪ Use of difficult-to-understand derivative financial instruments to hide fraud
Inventory	▪ Invent physical units of inventory ▪ Increase fictitiously the unit price of inventories	▪ Hide physical units of inventory ▪ Fictitious reduction of the unit price of inventories
Customers	▪ Invent customer balances ▪ Fraudulently reduce defaulting.	▪ Hide customer balances ▪ Fraudulently increase defaulting
Other Debits	▪ Invent debit balances	▪ Hide debit balances

FIGURE 6.2 Examples of illegal accounting manipulations to increase or reduce assets

	Increases of debt	Reductions of debt
Loans and Credits	■ Inventing debts with partners or with other creditors	■ Hide debts with partners or with other creditors
Provisions	■ Post fictitious provisions	■ Hide provisions
Pension Plans	■ Increase pension debt beyond what the regulation allows	■ Illegally hide or reduce pension debt
Suppliers	■ Inventing debts with suppliers	■ Hide debts with providers
Other Debts	■ Inventing debts ■ Consolidate subsidiaries by the global integration method without requirements for this ■ Use of difficult-to-understand derivative financial instruments to hide fraud	■ Hide debts ■ Not consolidate subsidiaries despite being obliged to do so ■ Use of difficult-to-understand derivative financial instruments to hide frauds

FIGURE 6.3 Examples of illegal accounting manipulations to increase or reduce debts

	Profit Increases	Profit Reductions
Income	■ Fictitious income ■ Post deposits as if they were sales ■ Sales at prices above the market price in order to deceive with companies that don't consolidate, with companies in tax havens or screen companies ■ Transfer reserves to income	■ Hide income and not post them ■ Post sales as if they were deposits ■ Sales at prices lower than prices outside the market in order to deceive with companies that don't consolidate, with companies in tax havens or screen companies
Consumptions	■ Stop accounting for consumptions ■ Expenses at prices below market price in order to deceive companies that don't consolidate or with companies in tax havens	■ Fictitious consumptions ■ Expenses at prices above market price in order to deceive companies that don't consolidate or with companies in tax havens.
Depreciations	■ Fraudulently reduce depreciations	■ Fraudulently increase depreciations

FIGURE 6.4 Examples of illegal accounting manipulations to increase or reduce profits

	Profit Increases	Profit Reductions
Other expenses	▪ Account for expenses charged to reserves instead of including them in the income statement ▪ Hide expenses ▪ Fraudulently account for expenses as investments ▪ Expenses at prices below the market price in order to deceive with companies that don't consolidate or with companies in tax havens	▪ Invent expenses ▪ Fraudulently account for investments as expenses ▪ Expenses at prices above the market price in order to deceive with companies that don't consolidate or with companies in tax havens
Provisions	▪ Fraudulently reduce provisions	▪ Fraudulently increase provisions
Impairment of assets	▪ Fraudulently reduce impairments	▪ Fraudulently increase impairments
Financial Income and Financial Expenses	▪ Incorrectly assessing the results generated in financial instruments or other assets (to transfer results from one year to another) ▪ Hide financial expenses ▪ Use of difficult-to-understand derivative financial instruments to hide fraud	▪ Incorrectly assessing the results generated in financial instruments or other assets (to transfer results from one year to another) ▪ Hide financial expenses ▪ Use of difficult-to-understand derivative financial instruments to hide fraud
Results from Subsidiaries	▪ Inflate profits from investees	▪ Invest losses from investees
Income Tax	▪ Do tax fraud to pay less taxes ▪ Excess of deferred tax assets in a company with many losses	

FIGURE 6.4 *(Continued)*

6.5 MAIN ITEMS AFFECTED BY ACCOUNTING FRAUDS

In order to assess the importance of the different types of accounting fraud, we have done a study on the affected items in 148 accounting frauds that we have identified internationally from 1980 to 2016 (see Figure 6.5). In this figure, it can be seen that of the analyzed cases, in almost all of them the manipulations modified the net result and the equity. Among the other items that have been most affected by the manipulations are sales, customers, operations with subsidiaries, and expenses.

Affected Item	% on the Number of Analyzed Frauds
Net result	98%
Equity	98%
Sales and other income	82%
Customers and default	55%
Operations with subsidiaries	43%
Expenses	41%
Inventories and impairment	21%
Financial debt	16%
Accounts payable	13%
Mergers and acquisitions	2%
Others	7%

FIGURE 6.5 Items affected by accounting frauds in a sample of 148 accounting frauds performed internationally from 1980 to 2016
Source: Author's own work.

GLOBAL FRAUD IN XEROX

We go back to Xerox. This company, founded in 1906, was one of the giants of document management and photocopiers. In the course of 2002, the company had over 80,000 employees all over the world.

The fraud became known in the year 2000 when the company acknowledged accounting irregularities in its Mexican subsidiary. The irregularities consisted in not posting impairments in customer balances due to delinquency. Due to this problem, the SEC began an investigation in the Mexican subsidiary and there it had evidence that from headquarters aggressive accounting practices to increase profits were encouraged. Also, the headquarters' and subsidiaries' management teams had an incentive system that awarded achieving profit targets.

Simultaneously, there was another occurrence that triggered events. James F. Bingham, who had been working in Xerox's finance department for 15 years, was fired. The reason was that Xerox's management, including the CEO, had for several years been giving his department instructions to ensure that the accounts reflected certain profit objectives and, for that, accounting frauds were done. When the

(Continued)

frauds in the Mexican subsidiary became known, Bingham couldn't take it anymore and reported what he considered to be global practices of the company and, therefore, it wasn't just a problem in Mexico. Immediately, he was fired with a proposal of compensation equivalent to one year of salary which Bingham didn't accept and reported the company to the courts. This circumstance became known to the SEC, which contacted Bingham. Immediately, the SEC investigated Xerox in the United States and worldwide, and it was then discovered that Xerox had inflated its profits for the years 1997, 1998, and 1999 through two manipulations:

1. Hide profits for a time and then post them in the year that they needed to be increased. It is a cookie-jar type of income smoothing. According to the SEC, this is a commonly used technique and that same year it was also discovered in Microsoft.

2. Anticipate the profits from long-term leasing contracts. It is another smoothing that increases profits from one year, reducing that of future years. The fraud consisted in inflating the current value of future charges using an unreal discount rate since it was too low.

In both cases, Xerox changed the accounting criteria in relation to previous years. Therefore, in addition to using illegal criteria, it didn't report the changes of criteria in the accounts and, hence, it failed to comply with the uniformity principle.

As admitted by the company, the goal of the manipulations was to achieve the earnings anticipated by analysts, not to disappoint their expectations. Figure 6.6 shows the evolution of Xerox's earnings per share, separating the earnings without manipulation, the manipulation, and the analyst's earnings per share estimates.

According to Figure 6.6, in the fourth quarter of 1997 the earnings per share without manipulations were $0.56. The manipulation was of $0.17 per share. The published total earnings per share were $0.71 per share and the analysts' estimate was $0.70 per share.

Shortly after, Xerox had serious problems and dismissed thousands of employees all over the world. The CEO was fired shortly before (in 2001, before the scandal became known) with a compensation of $25 million and was replaced by Anne Mulcahy. In the end, the SEC forced Xerox to reformulate the accounts and fined it with $10 million. Six of the firm's managers were also sanctioned, with $22 million.

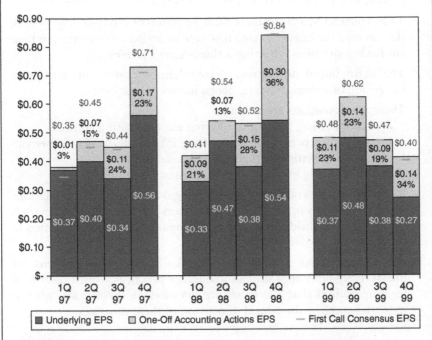

FIGURE 6.6 Evolution of the earnings per share declared by Xerox, manipulations, and analysts' earnings estimates
Notes:
Underlying EPS: Earnings per share without account manipulations.
One-Off Accounting Actions EPS: Accounts manipulations per share.
First Call Consensus EPS: Analysts estimates of earnings per share for the period.
Source: https://www.sec.gov/news/headlines/xeroxsettles.htm

In this case, the KPMG auditor had warned Xerox's management that these practices were illegal and also demanded they reformulate the accounts. However, the SEC considered that he should have done more when Xerox ignored the auditor's warnings.

Key Topics of the Chapter

- Illegal accounting manipulations are practices that aren't allowed by current legislation and therefore constitute accounting offenses.
- To be considered a crime there must be fraud. Fraud means lying with the intention to cause damage through an action or omission, to benefit from a situation, affecting a third-party's interest.
- The main illegal accounting manipulations consist in fictitiously increasing or reducing assets, debts, income or expenses.
- These manipulations are done:
  - By manipulating, forging or altering the accounting records.
  - Erroneously representing or omitting interesting facts or other significant information in the financial statements.
  - By intentionally misapplying the accounting principles.
- It is common for companies that do illegal accounting manipulations to make fictitious operations or post prices different from the market price through subsidiaries (or other companies) sometimes located in tax havens.
- Not all operations done with companies located in tax havens are illegal. Frequently they are tax-avoidance practices, which consist of legal operations that aim to reduce taxation. In these cases, what is more debatable is the ethical dimension of these practices.

REFERENCES

Blasco, J.J. (1998). De la Contabilidad creativa al delito contable. *Partida Doble* 85 (January): 34.

ICJCE (2015). Herramienta de planificación: "NIA-ES 240." *Instituto de Censores Jurados de Cuentas de España* (April).

King, N. (1998). Sark, "utopia" of English channel, faces heat for offshore havens, *Wall Street Journal* (July 16). http://www.wsj.com/articles/SB90054033 198468000.

Portillo, M.J., and Morales, F. (2015). Fraude fiscal y economía sumergida en España. Algunas consideraciones. *Gestión* 61 (July/December).

REA-REGA (2015). Documento técnico para la aplicación práctica de la NIA 240. *Registro de Economistas Auditores REA-REGA* (November).

Suozo, P, Sutherland, G, Cooper, S., and Deng, Z. (2002). *Can You Trust The Numbers?* Warburg, London: UBS.

CHAPTER 7

Ethical Considerations and Economic Consequences of Manipulations

Greed is good.

—Gordon Gekko (in the movie *Wall Street*)

7.1 THE ETHICAL DIMENSIONS OF ACCOUNTING FRAUD

Ethics means acting according to principles that are acceptable from a moral point of view. In the past, organizations were simply asked to reach their goals and, in the case of for-profit companies, to make money. An example is the Nobel laureate Milton Friedman, who in 1970 stated, "A company's social responsibility is to increase its earnings."

However, although many today continue to think like Friedman, society has become more sensitive to ethical issues. This is a consequence of trends like the greater diffusion of all types of information, scandals that have increased mistrust in many organizations, and the perception of companies' growing social responsibility. This increased awareness explains the increase in the number of organizations that launch ethical codes in order to promote ethics in the behavior of managers and employees.

Accounting frauds generate questions regarding its ethical dimension. There are those who question whether or not they are admissible practices. As shown in Figure 7.1, there are practices that are clearly ethical and others that are clearly unethical, but in the middle there is an ample gray zone where there is less unanimity when classifying them. When the accounting information violates the law, it is clear that it is an unethical behavior. This is also clear when it comes to frauds that seek to benefit the private interests of managers, for example, to receive a higher bonus.

Ethical	Gray Zone	Unethical
Respects the spirit and letter of the law. Realistic estimates. Neutral posting that are intended to reflect reality.	Respects the law, but uses alternative estimates. Self-interested estimates. Deceptions that are far from the truth to benefit the company and protect jobs (lying for good reasons).	Infringes the law. Unrealistic estimates. Lies to benefit private interests by hurting the company, its shareholders, or other interested parties.

FIGURE 7.1 Border between ethical and unethical actions

On the other hand, the practices that use estimates or alternatives allowed by the regulation, but that aren't neutral and don't seek to report the reality but rather are pursuing interested information, are dubious. Nor is it clear the ethical dimension when you lie "for good reasons" such as protecting the jobs of employees, for example.

The gray zone also exists when it isn't clear what the "truth" is on a given topic. For example, when you sell on credit to a customer, there is almost never an absolute certainty that it will be collected at maturity. In these cases, it isn't possible to estimate the risk of default in a single way that is "real" and current legislation provides an ample margin to estimates, which can be more or less neutral.

It is clear that deceits are wrong when they go against current legislation.

In the case of legal manipulations, we can find several positions. On one hand, it can be considered a fraud and, therefore, dishonest and intolerable, since it harms accounts users. On the other hand, some people consider justified lying for good reasons, like to avoid being denied credit. Machiavelli, for example, justified deceits if the purpose was good. So did Plato in the 380 BC when he stated in his book *The Republic*, "It is allowed to lie for the good of the community." This is what those who commit accounting frauds think. Anyway, there is a broad consensus that accounting fraud is immoral since it leaves shareholders and creditors unprotected. For those who justify deceiving for good reasons, we can remind them that account users have a right to know the truth about a company.

In most cases, the fraud is done to benefit those who lie at the expense of harming those deceived, whether investors, banks or the company itself that has had its numbers manipulated.

As explained above, legal accounting manipulation involves the distortion of the annual accounts, within the margins of action allowed by the legislation. At this point, it is convenient to compare this alleged dishonesty with illegal accounting manipulations. On one hand, there is a clear difference between the deliberate transgression of the law, and the actions, within the law, that we find in legal accounting manipulations. Anyway, there are two important points of coincidence between fraud and legal accounting manipulation:

1. In both cases there is the intention to mislead.
2. Often, both are the answer to the company's financial difficulties.

As a result, legal accounting manipulation, though not illegal in itself, is an indication of a situation where managers are under financial pressure and working below the highest ethical standards. Therefore, half-truths or lies, though merciful in some cases, could be interpreted as indication of unacceptable situations.

In short, accounting manipulations, whether legal or illegal, in most cases are unacceptable.

7.2   ECONOMIC CONSEQUENCES OF ACCOUNTING FRAUD

But beyond the fact you shouldn't lie for ethical reasons, accounting manipulations usually have disastrous consequences from an economics point of view.

In this section, it is argued that accounting frauds are counterproductive due to the negative economic impact it produces.

Accounting manipulation distorts the annual accounts and modifies the opinion on the financial information that users have (for example, investors, shareholders or banks).

Figure 7.2 shows the data of a study based on four companies that were found to have manipulated their accounts in 2012. The result for 2009 is on base 100 and, as shown, there are big differences between the declared results and the results without legal and illegal manipulations. These companies generated significant losses to shareholders and banks, so the economic consequences were disastrous.

Whether they are legal or illegal practices, since their goal is to distort the image offered by the accounts, it is a fraud that has very prejudicial consequences for those who suffer them. As an example, we can mention the study from Karpoff et al. (2008) that assesses in $150 million the losses caused to shareholders by the 585 American companies that between 1978 and 2002 were filed by the SEC for accounting manipulation.

7.3   CONSEQUENCES TO MANAGERS AND COMPANIES THAT MANIPULATE ACCOUNTS

When accounting frauds are discovered, there are also negative consequences for the companies and managers themselves. According to the aforementioned mentioned study by Karpoff et al. (2008) done with a sample of companies that were object of accounting manipulations, it concludes

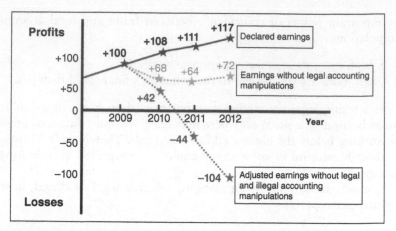

FIGURE 7.2 Example of impact of accounting manipulations in the earnings of four companies
Note: Study based on four companies in which it was discovered in 2012 that they had done legal and illegal accounting manipulations.
Declared earnings: are the earnings including the legal and illegal manipulations.
Earnings without accounting manipulations: are those that would have been obtained if the legal accounting manipulation hadn't been done.
Revised earnings without legal and illegal accounting manipulations: are the company's real earnings.
Source: Author's own work.

that the average price of these companies fell by 38% when the fraud was discovered. The main reason for the fall is the loss of reputation, but the deterioration of the future prospects of the company and the legal costs caused by lawsuits also have a negative influence. And from its managerial ranks, 91% were dismissed, 87% fined, and 14% ended in prison (remember we are talking about the United States). In addition, the loss of the affected company's reputation damages its future evolution, which causes the loss of jobs and in many cases ends in the company's disappearance, as it happened with Enron or Lehman Brothers, for example. It also generates distrust in supervising institutions. Other collateral damages are the discredit and possible penalties to auditors, in case they committed mistakes. In any case, it shouldn't be forgotten that often the first to be deceived are the auditors. All of these deceits damage overall trust in the system, which can slow down the smooth running of the economy and the financial markets. Thus, for example, when there is an accounting scandal of a listed company in a country, international investors start to distrust and lose interest in investing in the country. Given the negative consequences of these practices, it is of great interest to anticipate and detect them before it's too late.

Transparency, on the other hand, has positive effects. Several studies show that a greater transparency contributes to a higher rating and a greater disposition to invest in the company (Lev 2013).

7.4 WHAT TO DO WHEN A COMPANY DETERIORATES

How should one act when a company deteriorates? We have already seen the negative consequences of accounting fraud. Therefore, it isn't a good idea to hide bad results with deceits as, when they are discovered, it is much worse. Neither is it a good idea to conceal the company's poor performance with measures that may seem good in the short term but in the long term sink the company. An example would be when the company loses sales; it compensates selling to customers with low-credit ratings that in the medium term won't pay for the purchases made. This measure may sustain sales for a few months, but before a year or two the defaults will cause serious problems. A study by Lev (2013) shows that when a company has a problem, the best option is to recognize it, give detailed information about what is happening, and outline the measures to be taken to improve the situation. As it is often said, the best business is to be honest.

Fictitious Income and Other Illegal Manipulations at TESCO

Tesco, the British supermarket chain (the third largest in the world) admitted on September 22, 2014 that from 2011 to 2014 it inflated its profits by 598 million pounds with several accounting manipulations:

- Fictitious income: Tesco has agreements where the supplier pays them an incentive if at the end of each year they reach a certain volume of purchases. At the end of the year, Tesco posts an estimate of the incentives it will receive. The fraud consisted of posting exaggerated estimates of this income. This practice represented 27% of the total manipulation.

- Artificially overvalued inventory: This manipulation is related to the previous one, because to achieve a higher volume of purchases, they created an excess and part of the stock couldn't be sold due to obsolescence. This obsolescence wasn't reflected in the value of inventory and, therefore, the balance sheet value was overvalued. This practice represented 73% of the total manipulation.

Figure 7.3 shows the evolution of the declared earnings, the accounting manipulations done, and the adjusted earnings.

(Continued)

	2012	2013	2014	Total
Declared earnings	+2,814	+24	+970	3,808
Accounting manipulations	−150	−183	−165	−498
Adjusted earnings	+2,664	−159	+805	3,310
% Manipulations / Adjusted earnings				15.04%

FIGURE 7.3 Evolution of the declared earnings, the accounting manipulations, and the adjusted earnings

All these frauds were discovered due to the anonymous complaint of an employee from the accounting department.

Once the manipulation became known, the share price fell 40% over the following months and it still hasn't recovered (see Figure 7.4, where the arrow indicates the moment the scandal became public).

FIGURE 7.4 Evolution of the price of Tesco
Source: Google Finance.

As a result, the president of the company, Richard Broadbent, resigned and four managers were dismissed at the end of October 2014. In 2016, the British Financial Conduct Authority (FCA) imposed on the company a fine of 500 million pounds.

If we consider that the manipulated accounts weren't so different from the real ones, considering the disastrous consequences the fraud had to the company and the managers involved, the question we can ask ourselves is: Was it worth it hiding the impairment? Surely it would have been better for all to acknowledge the situation instead of trying to conceal it through frauds.

Olympus and the Top Management That Ended in Prison

Michael Woodford, ex-general manager of Olympus, a producer of photographic material, reported on 14 October 2011 the irregularities done by the company during almost 20 years.

The manipulations started in the 1980s, when Olympus was strongly affected by the fall of the yen. From that moment, Olympus's financiers tried to recover the losses with speculative transactions with foreign currencies that produced the opposite effect and the losses increased even more. During the 1990s, the losses caused by these transactions reached $1.7 million.

Initially, the losses were covered up using a Japanese accounting standard that allowed financial assets to be accounted for at historic costs instead of being valued at market price (when this was inferior). In 1997, the Japanese accounting standard was modified adopting the fair value as part of the implementation of the International Financial Reporting Standards (IFRS). Those in charge of the accounting knew that they would be forced to disclose the real value of the deteriorating assets they had. Therefore, in 1998, with the approval of President Kikukawa, they used several practices to hide the losses.

- Transference of assets without value to companies that they wouldn't consolidate the accounts with in the financial statements of Olympus. For this, they created several shell companies in the Cayman Islands using funding from a Liechtenstein bank.
- Purchase of companies paying prices well above the market price. Sellers received a surcharge with the condition that part had to be destined to pay the loans that the shell companies had received.

The first warnings of these frauds arrived in 2009 when the auditor KPMG detected that the companies bought by Olympus were recorded at values much higher than the real ones. On September 29, the British executive Michael Woodford, who had been in the company for over 30 years and was responsible for Olympus in the United Kingdom, was assigned to Tokyo and named general manager to cut company expenses. Shortly after, Woodford claimed the position of CEO to investigate the case due to some leaks he received about dubious financial movements of the company. In face of the incongruities found, he commissioned PriceWaterhouseCoopers

(Continued)

(PwC) to investigate the transactions that raised suspicions. When he discovered the magnitude of the problem, he requested the board of directors to dismiss Kikukawa. Immediately, Woodford was dismissed under the justification of not understanding the Japanese management style. Woodford immediately returned to London since he feared for his life and started to tell what he knew to journalists and regulators and even wrote a book telling with excruciating detail everything he knew. Very critical with what he discovered, he includes pearls in his book such as: "There is a system of shareholding crosses, and an incestuous relationship between companies, providers and banks. Many Japanese companies have mediocre boards or something worse and they continue in that position until they retire. With a public debt above 200% of the GDP, Japan needs a vibrant corporate sector, but all it gets are unedifying power games, played behind closed doors by a small elite."

Finally, and after a long fight, in 2013 President Kikukawa, the vice president, and the internal auditor were sentenced to three years in prison. During those years, Olympus' shares suffered several setbacks, especially in 2008, 2009, and 2011, as the frauds became public.

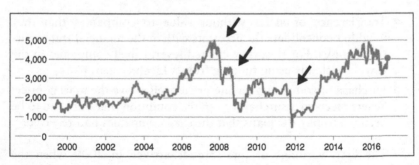

FIGURE 7.5   Evolution of Olympus' price from 2000 to 2016
Source: Google Finance.

In this case, the negative consequences (prison, sinking of the company's shares) of not acknowledging the problems immediately are proven and also that often there are people who risk their lives when they don't accept to play into the hands of fraudsters.

Key Topics of the Chapter

- Ethics means acting according to the acceptable principles from a moral point of view.
- Although some people justify lying for good reasons, manipulations are ethically reprehensible.
- Accounting manipulation, whether legal or illegal, is a scam, so in most cases, it is unacceptable. It is clear that shareholders and other users have a right to know the truth about the company.
- There are practices that are clearly ethical and others that are clearly unethical, but in between there is a large gray area where there is less unanimity when classifying accounting practices.
- Accounting manipulations can have serious consequences: the company's loss of value and reputation, legal costs, dismissal of executives, fines, and even jail, when it comes to accounting crimes.
- Greater transparency leads to a higher valuation of the company and a greater willingness to invest in it.
- When a company deteriorates, it is best to expose it as soon as possible and propose measures to correct the situation. This is recommended not only for ethical reasons, but also for economic reasons and to avoid other negative consequences (jail, dismissals, and so on).

REFERENCES

Friedman, M. (1970). The social responsibility of business is to increase its profits. *The New York Times Magazine* (September 13).

García, M.A., and Maestro, C. (2012). Hacia una norma de auditoría sobre responsabilidad del auditor ante el fraude. *Partida Doble* 240 (February).

Gowthorpe, C., and Amat, O. (2005). Creative accounting: Some ethical issues of macro- and micro-manipulation. *Journal of Business Ethics* 57 (1): 55–64.

Karpoff, J., Lee, S., and Martin, G. (2008). The consequences to managers of financial misrepresentation. *Journal of Financial Economics* 88: 193–205.

Lev. (2013). *Ganar la Confianza de los Accionistas*. Barcelona: Profit.

International Federation of Accountants. (2013). Responsabilidades del auditor en la auditoría de estados financieros con respecto al fraude. *Norma Internacional de Auditoría* 240.

Machiavelli, N. (1998). *El Príncipe*. Madrid: Tecnos.

Plato. (2004). *The Republic*. Indianapolis: Hackett.

CHAPTER 8

Personal Warning Signs

Mr. Madoff is one of the masters of the New York Stock Exchange.
—Wall Street Journal, 1992

In this chapter we begin the part of the book that tries to identify warning signs that help prevent or uncover accounting frauds before it's too late. A warning sign is a red flag that warns you should go with precaution. Depending on the importance of the warning sign or the number or warnings detected, we could consider it a sign that a company has to be investigated more in depth due to the high probability that an accounting manipulation will occur or has already occurred.

The clearest warnings signs regarding manipulations are in the accounts, as will be discussed later. However, there are also warning signs related to the people, to the company, or to nonfinancial indicators that are very useful to detect accounting frauds.

Without a doubt, auditors are the ones who have access to more of the companies' information that can provide warning signs. Anyway, let's not forget that most companies aren't audited. In any case, anyone interested (investors, bank analysts, etc.) must pay attention to the signs that indicate fraud or the probability of a fraud occurring (Du Plessis and Koornhof 2000).

The problem is that in many cases no one pays attention to the warning signs. According to KPMG (2013a), in 21% of the frauds, there were very clear warning signs that a fraud could occur or that it had already occurred and were ignored.

8.1 MOMENTS THE WARNING SIGNS OCCUR

If we consider temporality, warning signs can be perceived (see Figure 8.1):

- **Before the fraud is committed:** These are aspects that increase the probability of the fraud occurring and are usually related to the

	Warning Signs that Anticipate a Fraud				Warning Signs that an Accounting Fraud may have Occurred
	Motivation	Opportunity	Rationality	Profile of Person or Company	
Person (Chapter 8)	Manager wants to collect bonuses.	Executive with conflict of interest.	Person who considers him/herself underpaid.	Luxurious lifestyle.	Changes in managers' habits.
Organization (Chapter 9)	Company needs to get a loan.	Defective control.	Unethical management.	Company that has a lot of ostentation and sumptuary expenses.	Problems with auditors.
Non-financial Indicators (Chapter 10)	Loss of clients or lower sales in physical units.		Layoffs are occurring.	The number of stores, or square meters of stores or factories are reduced.	Discrepancies between operational indicators (number of employees, stores, etc.) and sales.
Annual Accounts (Chapter 11)	Heavily indebted company.		If the company doesn't get financing, it will have to fire employees which will harm many families.	Sales and/or profits decrease.	Discrepancies between profit and cash.

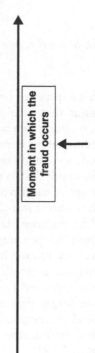

Moment in which the fraud occurs

FIGURE 8.1 Types of warning signs before and after accounting fraud occurs

motivation and the opportunity. For example, in a company that has a very aggressive incentive system for management that rewards profits, there is strong pressure to manipulate the results. And if control mechanisms in that company are deficient, it provides the opportunity for fraud to occur. In this case, we would be dealing with a company in which there is a higher probability of befalling accounting frauds.

- **After the fraud was committed:** Once the fraud has been committed, the warning signs are mostly quantitative and can be perceived in the accounts (see Chapter 9). That would be the case of an exaggerated and unjustified increase of customer balances that could be due to fictitious sales or to customers with low credit ratings. There are also qualitative signs that can be perceived after a fraud is committed, such as managers who lead a very luxurious lifestyle that isn't consistent with their salary.

Although a wide variety of warning signs are proposed below, it must be acknowledged that in practice detecting frauds isn't easy. In fact, most are discovered through anonymous complaints or by coincidence. According to Olcina (2016) and ACFE (2016), 42% of frauds are discovered after a tipoff (mostly from employees, customers, or anonymous people), 16% are discovered by the controls of the company's management, 14% through internal audit, 3% through external audit, and the rest (25%) are discovered by chance.

Next, warning signs related to people are presented. To recognize this warning signs, and thus detect frauds, it is very important to pay attention to details, especially those practices that aren't clear or aren't very logical.

8.2   WARNING SIGNS BEFORE FRAUD OCCURS

Remembering the concept of the door to fraud, we can recognize multiple warning signs that can inform us when the fraud hasn't yet occurred.

Motivation

- People who need more money because they have serious addictions (drugs, gaming, alcohol, sex, etc.) or because of their financial situation (many debts, high spending rate, etc.).
- People who want to collect bonuses with very aggressive objectives.

Opportunity

- Executives who have close relations or conflict of interests with suppliers or company's customers.

- People with seniority in the company who inspire a lot of trust, which explains why they assume many responsibilities and have less controls. A similar situation may occur with the owners' relatives. In fact, many frauds are committed by the owners' relatives.

Rationality

- People who consider themselves underpaid.
- Demotivated managers or employees.

Profile of the Person

People can have characteristics that increase the probability of frauds occurring.

The people who commit most accounting frauds are usually the chief executive of the company in collaboration with administration, accounting and financial managers. According to the Committee of Sponsoring Organizations (COSO), an international organization that fights business fraud, studies compiled by Beasley (1996) show that 72% of accounting frauds included the participation of the CEO and/or the general manager. A more recent study (ACFE, 2016) shows that executives or owners of companies commit 66% of frauds.

According to research conducted by KPMG (2011 and 2013b) on frauds committed in companies, the people who commit frauds have the following profile:

- 79% are men.
- 68% are between 36 and 55 years old.
- 65% work in the affected company.
- They work preferably in the administration and finance department.
- They occupy managerial positions.
- They usually have a seniority of more than 10 years in the company.
- In 62% of cases, they commit fraud in collaboration with another person.
- The motivation for the fraud is greed or the pressure to meet difficult budgets.
- 75% of frauds occur in a period that goes from 1 to 5 years, and it takes time to be discovered.

Let's look at other characteristics to take into account:

- Managers with histories of fraud in companies they have previously worked in.

- People with a very luxurious life-style.
- Very egoistical, authoritarian, aggressive and/or unscrupulous leaders who incite unethical behaviors from their managers or employees to please them.
- Leaders who continuously appear in the media.

The Birthday Party of Tyco President's Wife

This company caused another of the great scandals after the burst of the internet bubble in 2000. The fraud consisted of inflating corporate profits from 1996 to 2000 by 500 million dollars, and in the theft of 150 million dollars by President Dennis Kozlowski and the CFO Mark Swartz.

The profit was inflated through fictitious sales. The theft consisted of paying bonuses when actually the company had losses, as well as loans granted to the president that were never returned.

The SEC discovered the fraud after detecting illegal loans to the president. Shortly before, he had gifted his wife with a birthday party that cost over 2 million dollars.

The president was sentenced to 25 years in prison and the CFO to 8 years in prison. The company had to compensate its shareholders with 2.92 million dollars.

The Extravagant Lifestyle of Joseph "Joe" Gregory, President of Lehman

Joe was made to resign a few months before Lehman Brothers' bankruptcy, when the first losses were made public. His extremely expensive lifestyle stood out for being extravagant. For example, he travelled on his own helicopter to go from his Long Island house to Lehman's offices in New York. Shortly before he resigned, he charged hundreds of thousands of dollars by way of a bonus, and a year after the bankruptcy he demanded to be paid another 200 million bonus and uncollected rights.

8.3 WARNING SIGNS AFTER THE FRAUD OCCURS

Other signs can become evident after a fraud occurs:

- Executives or employees that lead a lifestyle with too many luxuries that do not match their income level.

- People who experience significant changes in lifestyle, or change of housing, expensive clothing, jewelry, luxury vacations, etc.
- Employees who don't go on vacation. It could be a sign they don't want other people to do transactions they do that can lead to discovering fraud.
- Leaders resist giving information to the media or they answer with evasive answers to specific questions related to the progress of the company.
- The language used by the leaders of the company (see Figure 8.4).
- Key managers leave the company without the reasons being clear.

Jeffrey Skilling's Departure from Enron

A few months before the great fraud was discovered, Jeffrey Skilling left the company. The motive he claimed: personal reasons.

Luxury in Vitaldent, the Chain of Dental Clinics

On February 17, 2016, the EFE network reported that a judge was sending to prison without bail the owner of Vitaldent: "As it is stated in the arrest warrant, Vitaldent's top management received each year 17.2 million euros in 'B' only from the 146 clinics owned by the chain. The magistrate considers proven that a group of people, among them the owner, had designed a complex fraudulent system towards franchisors, customers and patients and the Treasury itself. In addition, this company's activities had generated an enormous amount of opaque money originated from an accounting B."

According to *Expansión* (2016), this chain was created by Ernesto Colman in 1991 in Madrid. Initially it produced dental pieces and shortly after he opened the first clinic in the neighborhood Chamberi in Madrid. He created a model of success based on accessible prices to get to the general public. A sample of his success is that it was part of *Marca España*. Ernesto Colman became a regular on the lists of big Spanish fortunes. *Forbes* estimated his fortune at 550 million euros.

After two decades of spectacular growth, in 2016, the police (Unit of Economic and Fiscal Delinquency) arrested Ernesto Colman (president), Bartolo Conte (vice-president), and 11 other executives. The arrest was due to the alleged crimes of tax fraud, fraudulent accounting, money laundering, and scamming his franchisees and patients.

The police investigation started from the complaints that some franchisees were alarmed by being requested to make payments in cash of 10% of the fee they had to pay, which were collected in person.

Vitaldent came to have 450 centers (174 in property and the rest in the form of franchises) and 7,500 employees, of which 3,500 were dentists. Most of the centers were in Spain (364) and Italy (83). Other countries where it had centers were Poland, Portugal, and United States.

According to Expansión (2016): "The procedure followed by the plot was to divert the money received in cash outside of Spain, specifically to Switzerland and Luxemburg. Then that money was reinvested again in Spain. It was done with luxury articles, or they created new businesses... The prisoners had over 200 ranches, high-end cars, pureblood horses, two SICAV and an airplane rental company."

Also according to Expansión, among the possessions was a private airplane, a farm with horses in Segovia, 36 luxury cars, luxurious cottages in the most exclusive residential areas of Madrid, an attic in Manhattan, a whole town (Montgarri) in Vall d'Arán, etc.

Another characteristic was the complex corporate structure directed from Luxemburg (Dental International, company controlled by Ernesto Colman). This company, in turn, controlled Luxembourgish Dental Finance, which in turn controlled the company US Mississippi Invers, which in turn controlled the company Laboratorio Lucas Nicolás, which was the franchisor of the chain of clinics.

In short, among the warning signals would be payments in cash, complex corporate structures, companies in tax havens, and ostentatious luxuries.

8.4 LANGUAGE OF FRAUDSTERS

The language used by managers on their appearances before the media can also offer indication of manipulations. For example, when managers give evasive answers to concrete questions regarding the company's present situation. Or when they use intermediate margins (such as EBITDA, cash flow, or similar) instead of the net result when asked about the profits generated by the company.

According to Lillian Glass (2013), a specialist in the analysis of behavior and body language and a collaborator with the FBI, there are 10 signs, most of them nonverbal, to alert you that people might be lying when they talk:

1. They change the position of the head very quickly when answering questions or they remain too rigid.
2. They breathe more deeply.
3. They repeat words or sentences; it's a way to gain time to verify that what they say is coherent.
4. They provide too much unrequired information.
5. They touch their mouths when they talk.
6. They instinctively protect vulnerable parts of their body (neck, head, abdomen, etc.).
7. They move their feet, it's a sign that they want to leave.
8. It's hard for them to talk, because the stress situation makes their nervous system secrete less saliva.
9. They look more intently than usual at their interlocutor. Other experts indicate that liars avoid looking into their interlocutor's eyes.
10. They tend to point more with a finger.

Another sign that may betray a lying manager is that they seem to relax when questions change or the presentation changes to a less compromised topic. It can also be suspicious when verbal communication isn't consistent with nonverbal communication (gestures, looks, etc.).

A study with over 30,000 press wheels of presidents or CFOs (Larcker and Zakolyukina, 2012) concluded that lies can be discovered by analyzing verbal communication (essentially words). Managers who lie:

- Use more generic terms and less specific words.
- Refer less to creating value for shareholders, possibly to avoid lawsuits.
- Use more superlative words, for example, "fantastic" or "amazing" instead of "good."
- Use less "I" and talk more in the third person to distance themselves from the problems.
- Make fewer language mistakes and use fewer fillers like "er" or "ah." One explanation is that they take longer to prepare the intervention as well as the answers to possible questions.
- Use more bad words, insults, etc. especially when asked tough questions.

Other verbal signs could be perceived when they don't clearly answer the questions asked.

An example of the importance of language as an indicator of accounting fraud is that the American SEC uses software that detects signs of probability of fraud in the language used by the managers of companies (Eaglesham 2013).

8.5 SUCCESSFUL BUSINESSMEN WHO END UP IN JAIL

A phenomenon that never ceases to surprise us is the number of successful businessmen who end in prison. We can recall some cases of people who were awarded businessmen of the year and then, after crimes and accounting frauds, among others, were discovered, were sentenced to prison in the same year (see Figure 8.2).

This coincidence of awards and crimes can also be found in most of the big international financial scandals.

- Calisto Tanzi, president of Parmalat, received the Cavaliere del Lavoro award in 1984 and Cavaliere di Gran Croce Ordine al Merito de la República Italiana award in 1999 by the President Giorgio Napolitado.
- Richard Fuld, president of Lehman Brothers, was businessman of the year in the US in 1987.
- Ken Lay, president of Enron, was named businessman of the year by the Stanford Business School Alumni Association a few years before 2001, when Enron went bankrupt.
- Andrew Fastow, CFO of Enron, received the 2000 US Chief Financial Officer award, a year before Enron's bankruptcy.

Given this peculiar development of many successful businessmen, we can highlight a pattern that is often repeated. These are aspects related to what was shown in the theory of the door to fraud (motivation, opportunity, rationalization, and profile).

- In the beginning the entrepreneur manages, with a lot of effort, to create an innovative and high-growth company.
- Soon after he is a renowned businessman and gets all types of compliments and awards.
- They are people with a tendency toward egocentricity and overexposure to the media.
- Many politicians want to be close to them (and vice versa).
- Success makes them drunk.
- Excess of diversification and acquisition of other companies that are disastrous.
- When the first negative results appear, instead of acknowledging them and taking measures, they opt to manipulate the accounts.
- Operations with tax havens increase and the businessman steals money.
- Losses and debts increase.
- Members of the board sell their shares before they collapse.

Businessman	Position	Award	Crime	Sentence
José Vilá Reyes	President of Matesa.	Businessman of the Year 1969	Misappropriation of State funds.	In 1969 he was sentenced to 223 years in prison of which he served seven.
José María Ruiz Mateos	President of Rumasa.	Businessman of the Year on several occasions during the 1970s.	Currency evasion, fraud, threats, and misappropriation of funds.	As of 1985, he received multiple prison sentences, followed by absolutions, so that he was in and out of prison several times.
Mario Conde	President of Banesto.	Businessman of the Year 1987 (*Mercado* magazine).	Fraud and misappropriation of funds.	20 years in prison (2002).
Javier de la Rosa	President of Grand Tibidabo.	Several awards as model businessman during the 1980s.	Fraud, misappropriation of funds, and forgery of documents.	He entered prison on three occasions: between 1994 and 1995, between 1998 and 2000 and between 2002 and 2004.
Gerardo Díaz Ferran	President of *Grupo Marsans* and the Chamber of Commerce of Madrid.	Businessman of the Year 2006 (Cecoma).	Fraudulent bankruptcy, concealment of assets, integration in criminal group, and money laundering	Since 2012 he received several sentences. The last one was five and a half years in prison (2015).
José María Ruiz Mateos (segunda etapa empresarial)	President of Nueva Rumasa.	In 2009 he was again named Businessman of the Year by the newspaper *El Economista*.	In 2015 he went back to jail accused of punishable insolvency and fraud to the Public Treasury.	He was in prison on several occasions. He passed away in 2005 with multiple pending trials.
José Mestre	President of Tercat.	Businessman of the Year 2010.	Drug trafficking.	12 years in prison (2014).

FIGURE 8.2 Some Spanish businessmen of the year who later received prison sentences

- The scandal breaks out due to the confession of an employee or by suspending debt payments.
- Trials that end with jail and fines.

At the end of the cycle, many of these businessmen are forgotten, although some of them repeat their misdeeds. In other countries, especially the United States, some of these businessmen have been reborn as lecturers on topics related to, oddly enough, ethics.

Rumasa and Nueva Rumasa

We have already referred to this case in other parts of the book. Rumasa's great failure in the early eighties, which caused accumulated losses that exceeded 2 million euros and had to be intervened by the government, didn't stop José Maria Ruiz Mateos returning to create Nueva Rumasa, which attracted thousands of investors who invested in their promissory notes and lost their savings. Hundreds of suppliers of Nueva Rumasa and several credit entities that granted loans to companies controlled by Ruiz Mateos and family also suffered losses. And employees ended up not receiving their wages.

Some media (although not those top-rated) had been warning for years about the problems Nueva Rumasa presented. There were several negative signs. The accounting information presented serious reliability problems: audits with important exceptions that questioned the reliability of the accounts, lack of consolidation of the companies of the group that makes it impossible, even today, to have an idea of the real situation. Most of the companies were audited by different auditors, so there isn't an audit of the whole group. Nueva Rumasa's companies were controlled from abroad, which made it even more difficult. All of this shows important deficiencies of common sense, both from investors and, above all, banks.

In the cases of small investors it is more comprehensible because, perhaps, they didn't have the financial culture to adequately interpret the great amount of negative information that was being published. They let themselves be conned by the high profitability promised, between 8 and 10%, and by aggressive advertising.

Alfonso Ruiz-Mateos, one of José Maria's sons, in a trial held in October 2014, described his father's personality in the following terms: "Not only you didn't have power to decide but, many times, because of that overwhelming personality my father had, you didn't even have an opinion."

(Continued)

Parmalat: From Success to Jail Going Through the Cayman Islands

This case followed to the letter the fraud pattern. In 40 years, the Italian company Parmalat became a group with over 36,000 employees and subsidiaries all over the world. The president, Calisto Tanzi, was nicknamed Saint Calisto, for his economic miracles. His relations with the Italian Prime Minister Silvio Berlusconi were really close.

Then, the project leader got drunk with his success and started believing that everything he touched would become gold. That's the first mistake. It isn't the same being excellent with dairy products, than being excellent at the ruinous tourist division that Tanzi's daughter managed, or the Parma soccer team, where the company buried several millions.

The second mistake was thinking that you can steal money limitlessly. The millions Tanzi admits disappeared aren't supported by any company. He is accused of stealing around 500 million euros. As in other scandals, many of the fraudulent transactions were done through subsidiaries in the Cayman Islands. It is surprising that no one wondered what a dairy products company was doing with 7 million euros in the Cayman Islands. An example of the level of luxury that Tanzi enjoyed is that, after the scandal, in his residence were found hidden paintings of Picasso, Monet, and Van Gogh.

The third mistake was hiding that the company wasn't doing well. The profits fell and debts grew. Accounting manipulations and forgery of documents were done to deceive auditors and analysts. They simulated having multimillion-dollar deposits in the Bank of America, which were actually fake. Parmalat's accountants kept up to four different accountings. The fourth mistake was using privileged information and selling company shares before the scandal broke out. When, in 2003, the company couldn't face its debts, its price in the stock market sank. Then came the arrests, jail, shareholders' ruin, the loss of jobs, and so on.

Key Topics of the Chapter

- A warning sign is a red flag that warns you should go with precaution.
- Warning signs can be perceived before or after accounting fraud occurs.
- There are clear warning signs related to people that affect the motivation (e.g. people with too many debts or vices), opportunity

(e.g. people with a conflict of interest or with a very aggressive incentive system), and rationality.

- The most common fraudsters are men, aggressive and with an excessive ego, managers, middle-aged, from the administration and finance department, and with a seniority of over ten years.

- Greed and the pressure to meet budgets are usually the motivation to the fraud.

- There are other signals that can expose a fraud that has already occurred: people who have significant changes in habits, employees who don't go on vacation, key managers who leave the company without clear motives, etc.

- The language used by executives can offer clues of manipulation.

- Many successful businessmen end in prison for committing, among other crimes, accounting fraud.

REFERENCES

ACFE. (2016). *ACFE Fraud Prevention Check-Up*. www.acfe.com/fraud-prevention-checkup.aspx.

Beasley, M.S. (1996). An empirical analysis of the relation between the board of director composition and financial statement fraud. *The Accounting Review* 71(4): 443–465.

Du Toit, E. (2008). *Characteristics of Companies with a Higher Risk of Financial Statement Fraud: A Survey of the Literature*. Working Paper. University of Pretoria, South Africa: Department of Financial Management. http://www.repository.up.ac.za/bitstream/handle/2263/9141/DuToit_Characteristics (2008).pdf?sequence=1.

EFE. (2016). *La juez envía a prisión sin fianza al dueño de Vitaldent. La cúpula recibía 17 millones en 'b' al año*. (17 February).

Expansión. (2016). El fraude de las clínicas Vitaldent se eleva a los 10 millones. (16 February).

Glass, L. (2013): *The Body Language of Liars: From Little White Lies to Pathological Deception—How to See through the Fibs, Frauds, and Falsehoods People Tell You Every Day*. Pompton Plains, NJ: Career Press.

Du Plessis, D.E., and Koornhof, C. (2000). Red flagging as an indicator of financial statement fraud: The perspective of investors and lenders. *Meditari Accountancy Research* 8: 69–93.

Heiman-Hoffman, V.B., Morgan, K.P., and Patton, M. (1996). The warning signs of fraudulent financial reporting. *Journal of Accountancy* 182 (4): 75–81.

KPMG. (2011). *Analysis of global patterns of fraud. Who is the typical fraudster?* KPMG Forensic, Zurich. https://www.ub.unibas.ch/digi/a125/sachdok/2011/BAU_1_5663361.pdf.

KPMG. (2013a). *Perfiles globales del defraudador.* KPM Forensic, Madrid. portal
.protecturi.org/wp-content/uploads/2013/12/Perfiles-globales-defraudador
.pdf.
KPMG. (2013b). *A survey of fraud, bribery and corruption in Australia & New
Zealand 2012.* KPMG Forensic, Auckland. http://media.nzherald.co.nz/
webcontent/document/pdf/201311/Fraud-Bribery-and-Corruption.pdf.
KPMG. (2016). *Profiles of the fraudster.* KPMG International, Zurich. https://assets
.kpmg.com/content/dam/kpmg/pdf/2016/05/profiles-of-the-fraudster.pdf.
Larcker, D., and Zakolyukina, A. (2012). Detecting deceptive discussions in confer-
ence calls. *Journal of Accounting Research* 50 (2): 495–540.
Olcina, E. (2016). Motivaciones y perfil del defraudador en la empresa. *Revista de
Contabilidad y Dirección* 23: 11–26.
Padgett, S. (2015). *Profiling the Fraudster.* Hoboken, NJ: Wiley.
Pourciau, S. (1993). Earnings management and non-routine executive changes.
Journal of Accounting and Economics 16: 317–336.

CHAPTER 9

Organizational Warning Signs and Nonfinancial Indicators

In the business world, the rearview mirror is always clearer than the windshield.

—Warren Buffett

9.1   WARNING SIGNS BEFORE A FRAUD OCCURS

Using the door to fraud, we can identify warning signs related to the organization, before a fraud occurs.

Motivation

There may be managers interested in showing that the company is doing better than it actually is. This can be due to a number of factors:

- To avoid having difficulties obtaining financing.
- Companies with loans that have cancellation clauses. They are companies that have to accomplish certain requirements in their accounts (profits, debts, liquidity, etc.) to prevent a bank loan being rescinded in advance. In these cases, there is more pressure for the accounts to reflect that the conditions agreed on are met.
- Companies in which analysts and rating agencies' opinions are worsening.
- To avoid reprobation or dismissal, in companies that exert a strong pressure to meet certain goals or budgets that very ambitious.
- To receive a bonus. According to PricewaterhouseCoopers (2010), this is the main incentive to commit frauds in companies.

- When a manager is soon leaving the company, there might be interest in transferring problems to those who'll take the reins in the future.
- A company that has to be sold in the near future. In these cases, sellers may be interested in offering a better image that raises the selling price. This can also happen in the IPO (initial public offering).
- Companies that must comply with certain conditions (of purchases, sales, profits, etc.) to continue benefiting from certain contracts or licenses.

There may be managers interested in showing that the company is doing worse than it actually is:

- To pay less taxes.
- To curb the demand for wage increases or more dividends.
- To lower prices on dismissals.
- After a change in the board of directors or in the management team there may be interest in attributing problems to the previous management. In these cases, big baths are more frequent.
- A company that is object of tender offer. In these cases, if the shareholders that control the company are the ones who propose the tender offer, they may be interested in offering a worse image of the company to pay a lower price for the shares.
- Conflicts between shareholders or between members of the board of directors: In case of conflict, the group that exerts control of the company may be interested in hiding from the other side the company's true situation.

Opportunity

Defective Control
- Absence of internal auditing.
- Companies with internal control problems. In these cases, assets and information aren't sufficiently protected. According to KPMG (2016), 61% of frauds occur in companies with low levels of internal control.
- There isn't an adequate segregation of functions and there is a person who has the authority to carry through processes related to the generation of accounting information without anyone else's intervention. This causes one person to hold many functions, which favors fraud.
- Highly decentralized companies or ones with subsidiaries that are geographically separated and have defective control systems.
- Subsidiaries in tax havens with lower data requirements. Let's recall that the interest of operating through tax havens is not only in the

low taxation but also that the level of information disclosure is lower. For example, there are tax havens, like the Cayman Islands, where companies aren't obliged to keep accounting. Therefore, the unjustified existence of subsidiaries in tax havens, or an exaggerated number of these subsidiaries is a signal that requires attention. Enron, for example, had thousands of subsidiaries in the Cayman Islands, and it used them to conceal debts and inflate profits.

- Companies with very complex operations (triangular operations with other companies, significant number of subsidiaries, etc.), make it easier to hide certain operations.

External Control Problems

- Absence of audit of accounts.
- Unqualified auditor: An auditor who doesn't have the means to carry out the audit adequately or who doesn't know the business of the audited company.
- Absence of an auditing committee.
- Auditing committee with little preparation, that doesn't allow them to find out about the problems.
- A non-independent auditing committee because they are appointed by the President or are relatives of the president.
- Companies that have fewer controls because they stop auditing themselves or exclude themselves from listing on the stock exchange, for example.
- Significant transactions with related unaudited companies or audited by another auditor.

Governance Problems

- The president and the CEO are the same person.
- The president's family or friends are in the board of directors.
- Lack of independence due to a predominance of managers or directors appointed directly by the president. When these people are appointed, the real independence of the designated people is clearer. On the other hand, if the president makes the appointment, it could be people with a lower level of independence, who may favor looking the other way in case of fraud. In these cases, it is more feasible that the president or the CEO can act with more impunity.
- Presence of employees, former employees, or managers on the board. These are people that may have information about the fraud, but possibly don't have enough independence to report it.

A company with a high probability of unethical behaviors occurring. To evaluate this aspect, it can be checked whether it is a company that:

- Doesn't have ethical or conduct code.
- Doesn't have an approved document on policies in relation to frauds (from prevention to action once it has occurred).
- Doesn't have a channel for anonymous complaints. Therefore, if anyone detects a problem, he may be afraid of reporting it because of the consequences it may have.
- Has received sanctions for breaches of the current legislation in relation to consumers or in matters of labor, environment, etc.
- Is known for not acting correctly with some of the interested parties (employees, shareholders, creditors, community, etc.).

Rationality

There are also signs related to the rationality that warn that in a company it is easier to justify the manipulation:

- Company where the management sends unmistakable signs of being unethical, which makes the rest of employees think they can skip legality.
- Companies that need funding not to dismiss employees or close. In these companies someone might think that the manipulation is a lesser evil or that is justified lying for good reasons.

Profile

There are sectors and countries that are more prone to accounting frauds, such as:

- Companies in highly competitive sectors.
- Sectors that are experiencing a recession and business closures.
- High-volatility sectors where technological changes are frequent and relevant.
- Regulated sectors in which prices are set based on the results generated or forecasted: electricity, gas, highways, and so on.
- Companies that receive subsidies from the government to cover losses.
- Concession companies, where prices are set by the government. In these cases it is usual that the government analyzes the company's accounts to be able to regulate it, since it isn't the same for the company to be making profits or losses.
- Companies that operate in countries that are more prone to frauds (tax havens, etc.).

There can also be signs related to other characteristics of the company:

- Small to medium-sized enterprises (SMEs) and family businesses: In these companies there may be a higher interest in having low profits in order to pay less tax. Sometimes the manipulation is done to hide from minority shareholders the true situation of the company and/or to condition a certain dividend policy.
- Companies listed in the stock market: These are companies where there is more pressure for the profits to be high since, this way the evolution of the price will be more favorable. They can also feel pressured by analysts' profit forecasts.

Inflating Sales and Profits at Bausch & Lomb

Bausch & Lomb is in the optics sector (sunglasses and contact lenses). There was a scandal in 1993 when several executives inflated their profits by $17.6 million (11%). Following an investigation by the Securities and Exchange Commission (SEC), the company accepted to compensate its shareholders with $42 million and several managers were fined.

The fraud was committed by invoicing unsolicited sales to distributors that were returned on the following year.

In this case the motivation was a very aggressive, variable compensation system that pushed several executives to devise the fraud after failing to achieve the intended objectives.

In 2005 the company was involved in another very similar accounting fraud. Earlier, the CEO Ronald Zarrella admitted to having lied in his CV by saying he had an MBA from the New York University, which wasn't true.

The Madoff Fraud

When the 2008 global financial crisis of broke out, there were two major scandals that stood out among all others: Lehman Brothers and Madoff.

In 2008, when the fraud was discovered, Bernard Madoff managed funds worth $65 million. For over 15 years, his fund offered profitability to its customers that exceeded the market's profitability by an average of 6% annually. On average, it paid its customers a 12% annual return. Until the scandal broke out, Madoff paid investors with resources that were brought in by new customers, following the model

(Continued)

of the pyramid scheme. The losses he generated to his customers are estimated at $18 million.

Harry Markopolos was the first to alert about Madoff's fraud and reported it in the press, to the authorities, and also to the SEC in 2000, many years before the scandal was made public, but nobody paid attention to him. In fact, he warned the SEC five times between May 2000 and April 2008. Markopolos discovered it because the Boston firm where he worked asked him to replicate the same investment model used by Madoff. After studying it thoroughly, he reached the conclusion that the profits obtained by Madoff were fake and that it was a fraud. The warning signs that Markopolos (2010) focused are, mainly, the following:

- The profitability offered was consistently well above the market average every year. Madoff offered high returns both when the market went up and when the market went down. Fund managers have years in which they earn and years in which they lose. Madoff always won. During 174 months, his fund only had declines in seven (that is, 4% of the months). This is impossible, in the words of Markopolos: "It is as if a basketball player scores 96% of all shots." No manager has ever managed to overcome so much of the market and for so many years.

- His operation was opaque. Madoff never explained what his methodology consisted of. Shortly after the fraud became known, a manager from an important bank declared that they never invested on Madoff because when they went to see him and asked him to explain the methodology he used, Madoff refused to explain.

- Madoff had practices without any apparent logic and that were very different from his competition. For example, he didn't charge commissions for his management. No other manager did that. Usually in the sector you receive 2% commissions on managed funds and 20% of the profits obtained by the clients.

- Relatives in the most relevant positions. The company's key positions were occupied by Madoff (president) or direct relatives: his brother Peter (executive director and compliance director) and Peter's daughter, Shana (proxy and compliance officer). Madoff's sons, Mark and Andrew, also worked in the firm as salesmen.

- Only 28 people worked at the firm, which is an excessively small number for the volume of funds managed. It is an indication that in fact, the funds weren't managed.

- Given the volume of Madoff's manager, Madoff accounts were audited by a "peculiar" auditor. Friehling & Horowitz, a retired auditor with seven square meters offices and that in the past 15 years had only had one client: Madoff.
- Lack of segregation of duties. Madoff's manager received the funds from the clients, decided how to invest them, and guarded the funds and the securities in which she invested. Usually, different companies do the management and the custody of funds.

However, Markopolos' complaints to the SEC fell on deaf years. According to Peregil (2008), after Markopolos successive complaints: "Finally, in June 2006, the SEC opened an investigation on Madoff. That same year, Eric Swanson, a SEC middle-level official, met Shana Madoff, a granddaughter of the financier who works as a lawyer in Madoff's company. Swanson left his position at the SEC and last year married Shana. Shortly after, in November 2007, the SEC concluded its investigation stating that there wasn't evidence of fraud at Madoff's company. Some people wonder if the relationship of SEC's official Eric Swanson with Madoff granddaughter influenced something in the SEC's attitude." It was Madoff's sons who reported the fraud to the police. Mark stopped investing in his father's company in 2001, long before the scandal became public. After the complaint, a few days later Madoff confessed everything to the police.

After the trial a few months later, Madoff acknowledged the fraud. He confessed he's been doing it since 1990 and ever since the profits announced were inexistent. He was sentenced to 150 years in prison and to pay $17 million to his clients. His brother Peter was sentenced to 10 years in prison.

His sons weren't sentenced, since they didn't know about the fraud and, in fact, were themselves ripped off. However, two years later, Mark committed suicide by hanging himself on a pipe in his house.

But there were more suicides. The aristocrat Thierry Magon from La Villehuchet, financial advisor, cut his veins after losing with Madoff $1.4 million entrusted to him by several European multi-millionaires.

William Foxton, a war veteran, committed suicide with a gunshot to the head when he found out about Madoff's bankruptcy. All the savings from the Foxton family had evaporated.

9.2 WARNING SIGNS AFTER A FRAUD OCCURS

There are also signals that an accounting fraud may have occurred in the past.

- Companies with managers or employees more prone to fraud, according to the signs exposed in Chapter 8: lifestyle above to what would seem normal, financial difficulties, refusal to take vacations, excessive pressure from management, legal problems in the past, etc.
- Companies with a high turnover of key employees.
- Conflicts in the board of directors.
- Excess of luxury in the way the company operates, organized events, etc.
- Frequent changes in legal advisors.

Other signals are related to auditing.

- Tensions or conflicts with the auditor can be suspicious, since they are usually produced by discrepancies on the accounting treatment of some transactions.
- Voluntary change of auditor before the end of the contract or frequent changes of auditors.
- Hiding information from auditors: this may become apparent when the Management asks an employee not to give the auditor a particular information.
- Attempts to influence auditors' opinion.
- Inappropriate relationships between company employees and auditors, which could be signs of conflict of interest. An example would be romantic or family relationships.
- Conflicts because of discrepancies between members of the auditing committee.

Attention must also be paid to the emergence of problems with the authorities, such as:

- Tax penalties.
- Opening of a file by a stock market or other types of supervisors.
- Deterioration of ratings by rating agencies.
- Executives and members of the board who sell company shares without a logical reason, since they can foresee a significant fall in the value of shares.

INAPPROPRIATE RELATIONSHIPS OF AUDITORS WITH MANAGERS OF AUDITED COMPANIES

In September 2016, the American SEC imposed a historical fine of $9.3 million to an audit company because two of its associates had romantic relationships with managers of the companies they audited. It is the first time the SEC penalized this type of practices. In these conditions, the SEC considers the auditor cannot be objective in his work.

One of the partners, Gregor Bednar, 56 years old, was also fined with $45,000. His crime was keeping, from 2012 to 2015, an inappropriate relationship with the CFO (55 years old) of the audited company and he charged the auditing firm with expenses for 100,000 euros for gifts, travels, and sporting events. At least on one occasion the couple spent the night at Gregor's apartment.

Another partner, Pamela Hartford, 41 years old, fell in love with Robert J. Brehls, 54 years old, an accounting director from another company they were auditing. For years they kept a secret relationship (which was limited to an exchange of gifts and little else), which became public. The SEC fined her with a lower amount ($25,000) claiming that chaste love is a smaller sin.

The fine to the audit firm was because the SEC considered it didn't do enough to prevent and detect problems that generate a conflict of interest. According to the SEC, a third partner of the audit firm, Michael Kamienski, who was also fined with $25,000, knew about these inappropriate relationships and didn't do anything about them. Soon after these occurrences, all three associates from the audit firm and the two managers from the audited companies were fired from their companies. The SEC also penalized the auditors by removing their audit license for three years and one year, respectively.

The SEC found out about these events from a tipoff from an employee of the audit firm.

9.3 WARNING SIGNS BASED ON NONFINANCIAL INDICATORS

There are nonfinancial indicators that provide signals related to accounting fraud. These indicators can be warning signs when their values are very different from the competition or when they have no logic in relation to other company data or in comparison to previous years.

If these indicators have illogical values, the causes should be investigated, because they are not always due to manipulations, but regardless they might cause suspicions.

Commercial Indicators
- Sales/Number of stores
- Sales/Stores' square meters
- Sales/Number of employees
- Sales/Number de sellers
- Sales/Number of distributors

As Brazel et al. (2009) show, a very high value of these ratios compared to the competition, and without any logical explanation, could be due to manipulation. The previous ratios can also be used by putting the profits in the numerator.

Production Indicators
- Sales cost/Manufacturing square meters
- Sales cost/Number of employees

INCOHERENCIES BETWEEN NONFINANCIAL INDICATORS AND SALES IN DEL GLOBAL TECHNOLOGIES

The SEC fined Del Global Technologies for fraudulently inflating its sales. The fraud consisted of including products that still hadn't been manufactured, and products that were effectively delivered, but in later periods.

Several indicators gave warning signs that showed incoherencies during those years.

- While sales between 1996 and 1997 increased by 25%, personnel was reduced by 6.4% and the number of distributors was reduced by 37.5%.

- Fischer Imaging Corp., one of the company's competitors, announced a drop in sales of 27%, which was accompanied by a drop of 20% in the number of employees, and 7% in the number of distributors.

INCOHERENCIES BETWEEN NONFINANCIAL INDICATORS AND SALES IN ANICOM, INC.

Anicom Inc. was sanctioned by the SEC for fraudulently posting nonexistent sales. The warning signals were given by several indicators that showed inconsistencies during those years.

- Sales between 1998 and 2000 increased by 93%. During those years, several nonfinancial indicators also increased, but by substantially less: personnel (46%), number of stores (55%), and square meters (29%).
- Its main competitor, Graybar Electric Company Inc., on the other hand, had a very different evolution in these indicators. It increased sales by 11%, while employees grew 11%, stores 3%, and square meters 6%.

Key Topics of the Chapter

- There are organizational warning signs that warn us before (or after) a fraud occurs.
- Before the fraud occurs, certain signs can be perceived:
  - Related to the motivation: hide a deterioration of the company, obtain financing, improve the company's selling price, expose the previous management, and so on.
  - Related to the opportunity: defective control, lack of independence of the control entities, conflicts of interest, absence of auditing or an unqualified auditor, and so on.
  - Related to rationality: unethical management, and so on.
  - Related to the profile: economic sector with a lot of volatility or recession, operations with tax havens, family companies that want to reduce the payment of taxes, listed companies with more pressure to have high profits, and so on.
- And after a fraud occurs it is also possible to perceive signals, before it is too late:
  - Companies with managers that have lifestyles above the expected, conflicts in the Board of Directors, frequent changes in auditors or legal advisors, and so on.

- Problems with the authorities, fiscal sanctions, worsening of rating agencies' assessment, and so on.
- There are also nonfinancial indicators that warn an accounting fraud may have occurred: commercials, production, and so on. Therefore, it is convenient to analyze its evolution in time and compare it to the competition.

REFERENCES

ACFE. (2016). *The 2016 ACFE Report to the Nations on Occupational Fraud and Abuse*. Austin, TX: Association of Certified Fraud Examiners.

Albrecht, W.S., and Romney, M.B. (1986). Red-flagging management fraud: A validation. *Advances in Accounting* (3): 323–333.

Arnes, D., Brazel, J.F., Jones, K., Rich, J., and Zimbelman, M. (2012). *Using nonfinancial measures to improve fraud risk assessments, current issues in auditing*. American Accounting Association 6 (1).

Brazel, J.F, Jones, K.L., and Zimbelman, M.F. (2009). Using non-financial measures to assess fraud risk. *Journal of Accounting Research* 47 (5).

KPMG (2016). *Profiles of the fraudster*, KPMG International, Zurich. https://assets.kpmg.com/content/dam/kpmg/pdf/2016/05/profiles-of-the-fraudster.pdf.

Markopoulos, H. (2010). No One Would Listen: A True Financial Thriller. New York: Wiley.

PricewaterhouseCoopers. (2010). *Informe sobre los delitos económicos y fraude empresarial en España*. PwC Forensic Services, Madrid. https://www.stop-corrupcion.com/actualidad/publicaciones?download=19:informe-sobre-delitos-economicos-y-fraude-empresaria.

Saksena, P. (2001). The relationship between environmental factors and management fraud: An empirical analysis. *International Journal of Commerce & Management* 11 (1): 120–139.

CHAPTER 10

Warning Signs in the Accounts

There is nothing more deceptive than an obvious fact.

—Sherlock Holmes

A critical analysis of the accounts also allows the identification of warning signs. In most cases, the warning signs can be perceived after the accounting fraud occurred, although there are also warnings before the manipulation.

10.1 AUDITING OF ACCOUNTS

As mentioned before, auditing is not infallible, but the existence of a clean audit report is a good sign. If the report includes a favorable opinion with no exceptions, it means that auditors consider that the accounts have been prepared in accordance with the current accounting regulations.

Warning signs are produced if auditors issue an unfavorable opinion, or favorable but with exceptions. When the magnitude of the problems is very high and auditors don't have enough elements to emit an opinion, then they will refuse giving an opinion.

Let's remember the International Standards on Auditing ISA-ES-240 that indicates that it is the auditor's responsibility to obtain reasonable assurance that the accounts are free of errors due to fraud. Let's not forget that auditors can also be affected by the fraud. According to Calderon and Green (1991), the costs of defense, sanctions and compensations to be incurred by audit firms are relevant, accounting for 9% of their revenues. It is one more reason to use analytic procedures that allow evaluating warning signs and risk factors that could be an incentive to commit fraud (see Appendix 2 at the end of the book).

AUDITORS' WARNINGS CAME LONG BEFORE AFINSA'S BANKRUPTCY

This is a case of pyramid fraud. It was a philatelic investment company, just as *Forum Filatelico*, which compensated its investors with interest well above the market rates. To that end, it faked how the stamps were revalued. To be able to pay the high interests to investors it was necessary to exponentially increase the number of investors who were entering, since the new investors provide the money that allows repaying those who entered before. This way, it got 143,000 investors to trust in it. It operated like this despite current legislation that expressly prohibits chain or pyramid sales.

In Afinsa, there were enough signs of the fraud. Two years before the bankruptcy, which occurred in 2006, the auditors already questioned in their report the value assigned to stamps and indicated that the company hadn't provided them with key information, like the accounts of certain subsidiaries. These audit reports were public since they were deposited in the Commercial Registry. In the end, the people who trusted Afinsa lost a billion euros.

Indicator Related to the Audit

Audit expenses/Sales

A reduced value of this ratio, compared to similar companies, could be an indication of lower quality of the audit.

10.2 BALANCE SHEET

There are signs that can be found in the balance sheet:

- Assets outflows are concealed as loans from the company to associates or companies connected to them.
- Complex transactions in which it is difficult to understand the logic, especially when done with related companies.
- Assets for deferred tax for high amounts: These amounts are activated when losses occur, but they only make sense if there is the conviction that the company will generate profits in the coming years, since otherwise it is a fictitious asset.
- Noncurrent assets kept for sale: This item is sometimes used to increase the current assets and thus offer an image of more liquidity.

	Year 1	Year 2	Year 3
Increase in sales	5%	7%	8%
Increase in customer balances	6%	32%	59%

FIGURE 10.1 Evolution of the sales and the customer balances in a company in which an accounting scandal broke out during year 3

- Noncurrent assets contracted under operating leases with a contract that has a term similar to the useful life of goods. Being considered an operative lease, neither the assets nor the debts appear in the balance sheet, since only the installments paid as expenses are reflected in the income statement. However, by coinciding the term of the contract with the goods' life cycle, it could be thought that it is a financial lease and that, therefore, the assets and debts should be reflected in the balance sheet.
- Excess of accounting notes at the end of the year.
- Discrepancies between the variations in customers, inventory, or suppliers, in relation to the evolution of sales or purchases. Figure 10.1 shows the evolution of sales and the customer balances in a real company in which an accounting scandal broke out during year 3. You can see that from year 2, and especially on year three, there is a significant variation in the evolution of both items.

10.3   INCOME STATEMENT

The income statement can also offer warning signs. For instance, profits that are the result of accounting alternatives that have been used and the estimates with which the different income and expenses have been accounted for:

- Sales and/or the market share reduce.
- Orders reduce, which anticipates an upcoming fall in sales.
- High growth in sales and profitability compared to the competition without having a logical explanation.
- Significant sales to companies that do not have much logic due to the activity they perform.
- Inconsistencies between the evolution of sales and the profits or the cash flow (profit plus depreciations). For example, when sales reduce and, in turn, the profits increase.
- Sales that consist of nonmonetary operations. For example, an exchange of goods for advertisement; or an exchange of advertising for advertising, without any real movement of money. These practices can artificially inflate sales.

- Changes in the gross margin (difference between sales and merchandise consumption).
- A change in the expenses capitalization policy (R+D, financial expenses, etc.).
- Very conservative or very optimistic estimates about the value of the goodwill or of other assets.
- Changes in the revenue and expense recognition policy (depreciations, impairments, provisions, etc.).
- Accounts for expenses and losses charged to reserves (impairment of the goodwill, depreciation of assets, risk provisions, pensions, etc.), instead of including them in the income statement.
- Insufficient impairment of assets (bad debts, lawsuits).
- Hired services that don't generate a tangible or logical result.
- Reduction of profits for losses that will occur in the future.
- Accelerated depreciations.
- Changes in discretional expenses (noncompulsory expenses such as representation expenses, customer services, etc.).
- Exceptional income and expenses: Significant balances of items, such as the result for the sale of properties, or the restructuring of expenses or profits for the elimination of debts.
- Sale of assets below its market price.
- Discontinued activities: Profits or losses for this category.
- Not reflecting the expense of *stock options*. When an employee is granted a stock option, it is a staff expense that must be accounted for.
- Extraordinary contributions to pension plans.
- Dubious operations or excess of operations with related parties.
- A great amount of complaints to insurance companies due to loss of assets.

A VERY COMMON CASE: HIDING LOSSES CAPITALIZING EXPENSES AND INCLUDING THEM IN THE RESERVES

This is a distribution company that, due to the 2008 financial crisis, experienced a significant reduction in sales in the following years. As a consequence, profits started to reduce.

Before the crisis, the company earned about 600 million euros per year. For example, in 2007 it earned 604 million euros. From that year, profits started to go down. In 2014 it declared a profit of 452 million euros, but in the audit report was included an exception that said:

> *The company has charged against reserves a total of 825 million by way of impairments of property and factory closures,*

> *which doesn't correspond with the criteria of the accounting standards. This circumstance doesn't affect the total value of the equity, but it does affect the result that should be reduced in 825 million euros.*

According to the exception stated, the real result without the accounting manipulation should be 373 million euros, since the expenses must be included in the income statement.

Declared net result (profits)	452
Expenses charged against reserves	825
Net result (losses) without manipulation	−373

Therefore, the manipulation carried out helped the company hide that it lost money in 2014. Given that this topic was included as an exception in the audit report, users of the accounts had information about the manipulation performed that went against the accounting principles.

10.4 CASH FLOW STATEMENT

While profit is a consequence of multiple choices between alternatives and estimates, cash is not as easily manipulated. For this reason, in the cash flow statement we can find signals like the following.

- The cash flow generated by the company reduces or the cash flow is negative.
- Differences between the cash flow (net income plus depreciations) and the cash generated by the operations (data that appears in the cash flow statement). When the cash flow is positive and much higher than the cash generated by the operations, it might indicate that the company has raised items such as customers or inventory.

     The differences between both magnitudes are due to notes that may be subject to manipulation, such as:
  - Variations in the inventory balance.
  - Variations in the customer's balance.
  - Variations in the supplier's balance.
- Deterioration or variations without logical basis between the cash generated by the operations (CGO) and the free cash flow (CGO minus the cash flow of the investments) (Lee et al. 1999).

WARNING SIGNS IN WORLDCOM'S CASH FLOW STATEMENT

One of the warning signs that could be perceived in Worldcom was the evolution of its cash flow statement, which experienced a significant drop in 2000, two years before the fraud was discovered.

	1999	2000
+ Cash generated by the operations	+11,005	+7,666
+/− Investments cash flow	−8,716	−11,484
= Free cash flow	+2,289	−3,818

There are also ratios that can be useful.

Ratio of Difference Between Profit and Cash

This ratio was proposed by Sloan (1996) and is calculated as follows:

Ratio of the difference between profit and cash

$$= \frac{\text{Net profit} - \text{Cash generated by operations}}{\text{Assets}}$$

The cash generated by the operation is obtained in the cash flow statement.

According to Sloan, when the ratio has a value superior to +0.10, it is a warning sign related to possible manipulations. The reason is that it reflects a high amount of difference between the accrued value and what has affected the cash.

Ratio of Difference Between Cash Flow and Cash Flow Generated by Operations

This ratio, also proposed by Sloan (1996), is calculated as follows:

Ratio of the difference between the cash flow

$$= \frac{(\text{Net profit} + \text{Depreciation}) - \text{Cash generated by operations}}{\text{Net profit} + \text{Depreciations and the cash generated by operations}}$$

The net profit plus the depreciations are obtained from the income statement. The cash generated by operations is obtained from the cash flow.

When the value is positive, it is a warning sign, which will be stronger as the value becomes higher. The reason is that it shows differences between the result and the cash generated.

Differences Between a Manipulating Company and a Non-manipulating Company

Figure 10.2 shows the data of two companies, one that doesn't embezzle and one that was subject of a big accounting scandal. You can see that in the company that embezzles there are important differences between the profit plus depreciations and the cash generated by the operations, which would be a sign of a possible accounting fraud. In addition, in this company, in the second year the cash was negative while the profit was positive, which would also be a sign of manipulation.

	Non-manipulating company Year 2	Non-manipulating company Year 1	Manipulating company Year 2	Manipulating company Year 1
Profit + Depreciations	+936	+914	+250	+210
Cash adjustments (variations in inventory, customers, suppliers, etc.)	−5	−4	−426	−144
CGO (cash generated by operations)	+931	+910	−176	+66
(Profit + Depreciation − CGO) / Assets	−0.3%	−0.2%	−9.3%	−3.2%

FIGURE 10.2 Differences between the profit plus depreciations and the cash generated by operations in two companies (one that manipulates the accounts and one that doesn't). Data in millions of euros

Real Example of a Warning Sign in the Cash Flow Statement (CFS)

Recently, a big accounting scandal broke out in a company that generated losses to its creditors, credit institutions, and shareholders. The company considerably inflated its profits with nonexistent sales and raising the value of its inventories. Figure 10.3 shows that from 2005 (seven or eight years before the fraud became public in 2013), there were already significant discrepancies between the cash flow (profit + depreciations) and the cash generated by operations.

(Continued)

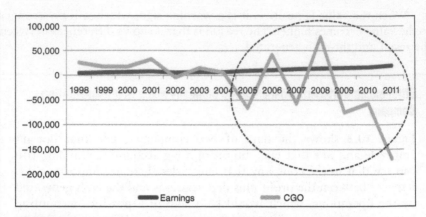

FIGURE 10.3   Evolution of the earnings (measured by net profit plus depreciation) and the cash generated by operations (CGO) in a company that committed an accounting fraud that later became public in 2013 (numbers in millions of euros)

The warning signs start in 2005, due to the discrepancy between the cash generated by operations (information included in the cash flow statement) and the cash flow (calculated using information included in the profit and loss statement). In 2010 and 2011 it is even clearer.

As previously stated, profits are a highly manipulable figure, since it is income and expenses. On the other hand, cash generated by operations is much harder to manipulate, since it is receipts minus payments.

Real Example of Two Companies: Company A (Non-Embezzling) and Company B (Embezzling)

Next, we show an example of differences between the cash flow (net profit + depreciations) and the operating cash flow of two real companies.

We know company A hasn't manipulated its accounts, whereas company B did manipulate them.

In company A we can see that the variation between both magnitudes on both years is very small. It is a company where no accounting manipulation was detected.

The case of company B is very different. Soon after year 2, it became public that the accounts from year 1 and, especially, those from year 2 were subject to a very high level of manipulation, which ended in a scandal of massive proportions since it was a company that had been hiding significant losses for several years.

Company A (Data in Millions of Euros and %):

	Year 2	Year 1
Cash flow – Profit + Depreciations	+936	+914
Cash adjustments	–5	–4
Cash generated by depreciations	+931	+910
Cash adjustments/Cash flow	–0.5%	–0.4%

Company B (data in millions of euros and % Year):

	Year 2	Year 1
Cash flow = Profit + Depreciations	+250	+210
Cash adjustments	–426	–144
Cash generated by operations	–176	+66
Cash adjustments/Cash flow	170.4%	68.5%

In the case of A we can see that the weight of the cash adjustments over cash flow is very low. On the other hand, in company B the adjustments are very high, which can be interpreted as a clear sign of manipulation of accounts.

10.5   STATEMENT OF CHANGES IN EQUITY

In this statement the company has to report circumstances that may be related to the accounting manipulation.

- Adjustments for changes in the accounting criteria. It is convenient to analyze the accounting criteria used, which are shown in the report that is part of the annual accounts. In the report you can also check if the company is doing any especial treatment authorized by the accounting authorities. As already mentioned, one of the accounting principles that companies must follow is the uniformity principle, which indicates that once an accounting criterion is chosen, it must be maintained over time unless the circumstances that justified the adoption of the criterion at the time changed. Therefore, when a company changes accounting criteria, it could be a sign of manipulation. These are, for example, changes in the depreciation policies, impairments, and provisions; or in the expense capitalization policy (R+D, etc.), or a change of inventory valuation system. These changes must always be explained in the report.

Anyway, it is worth remembering that in this case the auditor must also notify it in his report by making a qualification and quantifying the impact on the accounts.

It is necessary to contrast these criteria with those of previous years and those of competitors. This way you can identify changes in criteria in relation to previous years, or more (or less) conservative accounting practices than those of competitors.

- Adjustments for accounting errors. Accounting errors corresponding to previous years will be quantified in the statement of changes in equity.

10.6 NOTES

In the notes that are included in the financial statements we can also identify warning signs of manipulations.

- Lack of consolidation of subsidiaries: Another sign of manipulation is when a group doesn't consolidate subsidiaries with very close participations or that exceed 50% of the subsidiary's capital.
- High, off-balance-sheet operations with companies that don't consolidate. They can be, for example, guarantees granted to other companies.
- High, off-balance-sheet operations with nonrecourse debt: It is the case of nonrecourse debt that isn't placed on the balance sheet when the return guarantee is given by the asset itself that is financed and there are companies that choose not to reflect on the balance sheet neither the asset nor the debt. This is usually done with certain project finance as has been explained in Chapter 5. (Ketz, 2003). Debt can also be hidden through nonrecourse factoring, which is used when the company finances customers' receipts through a factoring company that advances the amount before the customer pays. It is a nonrecourse factoring when the company can't claim to the company if the customer doesn't pay at maturity. In some cases the company eliminates the customer debt from the assets of its balance sheet, and in the liabilities, it eliminates the debt with the factoring company. Therefore, the information of this operation can only be seen in the report. Depending on the characteristics of the operation, it may be debt concealment.
- Transaction without economic sense: Sometimes, manipulations are done through related companies performing unreal operations or at prices other than that of the market. Therefore, the operations with related companies must be analyzed.

10.7   RATIOS THAT ANTICIPATE FRAUDS

Multiple studies show that there are ratios that can anticipate frauds and ratios that are signs that a fraud may have occurred (Kaminski et al. 2004). Let's see the most useful ratios to identify companies with high probability of committing fraud. They are ratios showing that the company has problems with profitability or solvency. Because of these problems companies can have more incentives to manipulate the accounts.

Profitability and Margin Ratios

Özcan (2016) shows that companies with lower profitability and margin are more prone to accounting frauds. Therefore, the following ratios may be useful.

Cost of material over sales = Cost of materials/Sales

Margin over sales = Net result/Sales

Result on assets = Earnings before interest and taxes/Assets

Return on equity = Net profit/Equity

Liquidity Ratio

Insufficient solvency has also been identified as a sign of probability of accounting fraud by multiple studies that show that companies that have weak, short-term solvency and excess of debts are more likely to be embezzling companies (Du Toit, 2008). Given that companies with solvency problems are usually companies that sooner or later may fall into the temptation to manipulate accounts, it can also be used as signs the ratios that inform that a company has an excess of debts:

Current assets (CA)/Current liabilities (CL)

As the value of the ratio reduces and is less than one, it is more likely that the company has short-term solvency problems. This, logically, depends on the sector. For example, in the sectors that charge fast and pay later, like supermarkets, it is frequent that the ratio value is less than one and it isn't a problem.

Debt Ratios

Excessive debt is a very important signal, as is the continued refinancing of loans.

Debt = Liabilities (L)/Assets (A)

As the ratio value increases and goes over 0.60 or 0.70, it is more likely that the company has problems due to its excess of debt.

It is also dangerous when the financial expense increases.

Financial expenses/Sales

Financial expenses/Loans

Z-Score Formula

The Z-score formulas, originally proposed by Altman (1968), can be very useful to determine if a company has a higher or lower probability of having insolvency problems.

Let's see a model calculated from the analysis of a sample of 80,000 companies that are both solvent and that have insolvency problems (Amat, Antón, and Manini 2016). The model considers four ratios that are proven to be very related to insolvency.

- Ratio 1: Current assets (CA)/Current liabilities (CL)
  When it decreases, the company's solvency deteriorates.
- Ratio 2: Equity (E)/Assets (A)
  When it decreases, the company's solvency deteriorates.
- Ratio 3: Net profit (NP)/Assets (A)
  When it decreases, the company's solvency deteriorates.
- Ratio 4: Net profit (NP)/Net Worth (E)
  When it decreases, the company's solvency deteriorates.

The formula is as follows:

$$Z = -3.9 + 1.28 \times R1 + 6.1 \times R2 + 6.5 \times R3 + 4.8 \times R4$$

And it is analyzed considering that:

- Value above 0: increases the probability of the company not having solvency problems.
- Value below 0: increases the probability of the company having solvency problems.

As shown, when a company has a higher probability of having insolvency problems, it has a higher probability of committing accounting frauds.

Example on How to Forecast the Default of a Company

In Figure 10.4 we see the evolution of the Z score (Amat, Antón, and Manini 2016) of a company that was in default in year 8. As a value lower than zero means a high probability of default, we can conclude that in year 5

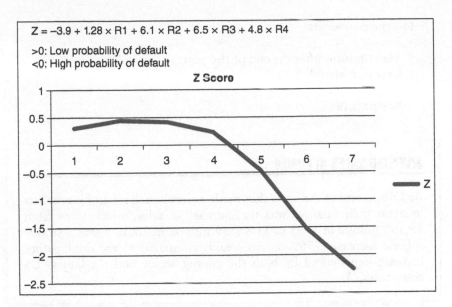

$$Z = -3.9 + 1.28 \times R1 + 6.1 \times R2 + 6.5 \times R3 + 4.8 \times R4$$

>0: Low probability of default
<0: High probability of default

FIGURE 10.4 Z-score evolution of a company that was in default in year 8

(three years before the default) it was possible to forecast the insolvency of the company.

10.8 VARIATIONS IN ACCOUNTS THAT WARN OF FRAUDS ALREADY PRODUCED

When there are significant variations that are not justified in the accounts, both in the balance sheet and in the income statement, you'll have to pay attention to them. We are referring to variations that are greater than the sales' variation, and also superior to what is happening in comparable companies.

Examples of accounts to consider could be the following.

- Balance sheet:
  - Expenses capitalized and included in fixed assets
  - Research and development (in countries where they can be capitalized)
  - Pending remuneration payments
  - Inventory
  - Customers

- Income statements:
  - Sales
  - Many returns after the end of the year
  - Cost of materials
  - Depreciation
  - Impairments

INVENTED SALES AT ENRON

At Enron, one of the signs that made several analysts and journalists mistrust their finances was the increase in sales, which went from $9,189 million in 1995 to $100,789 million in 2000. It was a stratospheric increase (996% in five years) compared to the double-digit increase experienced by both the energy sector and the largest US companies.

10.9   RATIOS THAT WARN OF FRAUDS ALREADY PRODUCED

Multiple studies conclude that ratios may provide clear warning signs that a fraud has occurred (Spathis et al., 2002). Among the most powerful ratios, the following stand out.

Term Ratios

Among the most powerful warning signs are significant variations in inventory, customer, and supplier term ratios.

$$\text{Inventory term} = (\text{Inventory}/\text{Cost of sales}) \times 365$$

$$\text{Collection term} = (\text{Customers}/\text{Sales}) \times 365$$

$$\text{Payment term} = (\text{Suppliers}/\text{Purchases}) \times 365$$

For example, if the collection term increases a lot in relation to that of the competition or in relation to previous years, it may be an indication that there is a lot of delinquency or of unrecognized impairments. The US Securities and Exchange Commission uses an automated computer system that verifies companies' accounts by comparing them with those of the competition to detect differentiated behavior.

Asset Turnover

This is another ratio that can give a signal of manipulation.

Turnover ratio = Sales/Assets

Once again, an evolution that is very different from that of previous years or from that of competitors may raise suspicions, if the change isn't justified.

Let's see two real cases that serve to verify the usefulness of the proposed signals.

Lernout & Hauspie Speech Products (LH): The Biggest Accounting Scandal in Belgium's History

Two entrepreneurs, Jo Lernout and Pol Hauspie, who previously worked in IT companies, created this company in 1987. Their dream was to supply computer technologies for voice recognition.

To finance the company, both partners sold their properties (Lernout sold his house; and Hauspie, his IT company) and they also got financing from family and friends. Later, they obtained financing from venture capital companies. In 1995, it started to list on the American NASDAQ and the technological market of the Brussels Stock Exchange.

Until 1998, LH generated negative results;1999 was the first year the official accounts showed profits (see Figure 10.6).

In 1999 it made multimillion-dollar acquisitions of competitors, like the American companies Dragon or Dictaphone (for which LH paid $690 million). These transactions in the USA aroused the interest of journalists and analysts who began to focus their attention on LH. In that same year, LH was experiencing strong growth in sales and profits, basically achieving it through its subsidiaries in Asia. In 1999 it stated that its sales in the South Korean subsidiary had increased up to $62 million and the Singapore subsidiary to $80 million, when the previous year it practically hadn't sold anything. These sales in Asia, more important than LH sales in the United States, raised suspicions since in Asia the level of investments was much lower (see Figure 10.7).

At the beginning of the year 2000, negative rumors about the company began to circulate. Robert Smithson, a Goldman Sachs analyst, published an article in the *Wall Street Journal* in which he

(Continued)

wrote that LH was inflating its profits. Later, an investigation by Jesse Eisinger, a *Wall Street Journal* analyst, revealed in August 2000 that LH did a good part of its sales through subsidiaries in South Korea and Singapore, and that they were presumably fake sales, since these subsidiaries operated with companies that had neither employees nor real operations.

Figure 10.5 shows the collapse of LH's share price from the beginning of 2000, when doubts about the company's operations and accounts began to appear.

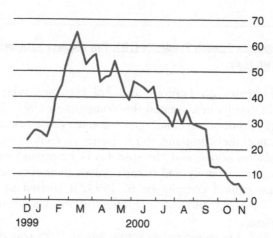

FIGURE 10.5 Evolution of the price of LH from December 1999 to November 2000
Source: Thomson Financial Datastream.

As a result of the SEC's investigations, evidence of accounting fraud at LH was found.

- Between 1996 and 1999 it made sales (worth $60 million) related to research and development projects that hadn't yet been proven to be able to succeed in the market. To do this, it sold to third companies that, later, were acquired by LH itself at prices that enabled to the owners of these companies the purchases they had previously made to LH.

- In 1998 and 1999 it did fictitious sales worth $109 million to several companies domiciled in Singapore. People related to LH managed these companies; they didn't have employees nor did they do real operations in Singapore.

- Between September 1999 and June 2000 it did fictitious sales through its subsidiary in Korea. To obtain liquidity and give the image that the (fictitious) customers paid for these operations, nonrecourse factoring from Korean banks was used (once the bank anticipated the amount of the sale to LH's Korean subsidiary, it couldn't claim this company in the event of the customer's default). Actually, the money anticipated by the banks was blocked in accounts that LH couldn't use. In this way, the bank covered the risk of default and LH gave the impression that the sales were real. A consequence of these operations was that the bank deposits that LH's Korean subsidiary had weren't actually available.

- Also during those years, in LH's Korean subsidiary, fictitious sales to third companies were registered. These companies paid LH with money that they obtained from bank loans guaranteed by LH. These guarantees weren't reported in the accounts.

- They posted fictitious sales and purchases (in the form of barter) with other software companies.

- Altogether, the amount of invented sales exceeded 70% of the company's sales in the years 1998 and 1999.

- In 1999, in the midst of these massive accounting frauds, the two founders of the company announced their decision to buy shares worth $40 million. This information increased the price of the shares by 9%.

When the results of the investigations of the stock supervisors became public, several events were triggered. In April 2001, Jo Lernout and Pol Hauspie (founders of the company) and Gaston Bastiaens (CEO) and Nico Willaert (vice president) were arrested. In October LH went bankrupt, causing a loss of value to its shareholders of $8.6 million. A few years later, the founders and the company's two main executives were sentenced to five years in prison for accounting fraud, stock price manipulation, and use of privileged information. The Belgian bank Dexia Bank and the auditor KPMG Bedrijfsrevisoren were absolved after accepting to pay $60 million and $115 million, respectively, to the American government.

In the end, in 2001, Nuance Communications Inc. acquired LH for $39.5 million. At its time of maximum splendor it came to have a market value of $10 million.

From the facts exposed, it is clear that there are some signs of the possible existence of some type of fraud.

(Continued)

- The inconsistency of the Sales/Assets ratio in Singapore compared to other areas in the United States and Europe.
- Astronomical growth of sales in Singapore and South Korea, not justified by the investment done in these countries.

These are the signs that enabled several analysts to discover the frauds committed by the company.

	1995	1996	1997	1998	1999
Sales	7,722	31,014	99,371	211,592	344,237
Cost of sales	−2493	−6,681	−38,770	−69,643	−94,255
Commercial, administrative, and general expenses	−11,172	−12,982	−26,042	−59,354	−101,641
Research and development	−4,920	−6,700	−6,393	−25,165	−49,621
Depreciations of fixed assets	0	−638	−6,809	−19,978	−32,439
Depreciations of R+D	0	−11,514	−33,823	−79,373	0
Other operating expenses	0	0	−1,453	−1,821	0
Income and nonoperating expenses	+3,112	−125	+812	+1,441	−7,111
Net Income	**−13,975**	**−7,376**	**−14,731**	**−45,183**	**+73,292**

FIGURE 10.6   LH's official income statements (data in thousands of dollars)

	Sales			Sales growth	Assets			Sales/ Assets
	1997	1998	1999	1999/1998	1997	1998	1999	1999
USA	26,524	79,695	79,286	−0.5%	52,273	117,115	128,032	0.61
Belgium	40,375	58,930	34,343	−41%	18,477	57,772	141,115	0.24
Rest of Europe	25,709	63,315	79,079	+24%	31,442	97,659	101,782	0.77
Singapore	0	29	80,297	+2,767%	0	5,434	5,169	15.5
South Korea	1,645	245	62,874	+2,159%	0	0	52,471	1.19
Far East	5,118	9,378	8,358	−11%	2,954	5,098	4,269	1.95
Total	**99,371**	**211,592**	**344,237**		**105,146**	**283,078**	**432,838**	

FIGURE 10.7   Information of sales and assets segmented by geographic areas (in thousands of dollars)

La Polar, the Biggest Accounting Scandal in Chile

La Polar was created in 1920 in Santiago de Chile and was a modest tailor shop. In 1980 it began to operate department stores. Over the years it experienced spectacular growth. It became a listed company and one of the biggest retail distribution companies in Chile, with 9,000 employees. Its success formula was to go to the middle and low classes with very low prices and provide credit cards to its customers that allowed them to pay for any purchase, no matter how small, in up to 48 months.

From 2008 (see Baires et al. 2011 and Wharton 2011), after the global economic crises began, La Polar evolved very favorably in sales and profits, while its competitors were registering losses due to the falls in sales, margins, and the increase of delinquency. The accounts of La Polar, on the other hand, weren't registering delinquency problems and the profits were increasing. From 2003 to 2011, La Polar's shares were revalued at more than 500%. Top management received incentives every year (see Figure 10.8) that represented 20% of the profits and the members of the board of directors 1.5%. In the competing companies, these percentages were much lower, 9% and 0.4%, respectively.

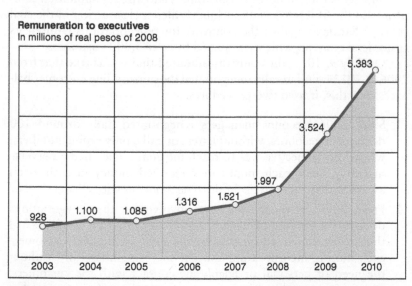

FIGURE 10.8 Evolution of incentives received by managers of La Polar
Source: La Tercera (June 26, 2011).

(*Continued*)

Meanwhile, stock exchange analysts, auditors, and rating agencies emitted favorable reports on La Polar. Between 2008 and 2009, the SERNAC (National Consumer Service) received over 300 complaints from consumers for malpractice in the renegotiations of delinquent balances of La Polar, but the complaints were filed without any resolution.

Shortly after, the scandal broke out. A few days earlier several events occurred:

- On June 3, 2011, a small firm of young lawyers presented a report to the SVS (Superintendencia de Valores y Seguros, supervisor of the Chilean stock market) about the inconsistency of its accounts in relation to those of the competition.
- The financial income received from customers represented over 80% of sales, when in the competitors this percentage was around 10%.
- The customer/sales ratio was much lower than its competitors.
- The delinquency/sales ratio was almost inexistent, while in its competitors it was much higher and growing.

Shortly before, hundreds of customers had already submitted complaints to the SERNAC that, on June 2, filed a class action in the civil court of Santiago against the company for renegotiations without its customers' consent, which was joined by over 5,000 customers.

On July 9, 2011, the company admitted that it was true that from 2006 to 2011 it unilaterally renegotiated the outstanding customer balances. For this, it used two procedures:

1. Since 2006, account managers renegotiated daily around 100 delinquent accounts, without letters or calls, only typing numbers, whose only objective was to reach the goals. They had a perverse incentive, since each month they received money in cash as an award if they met targets in the renegotiation with clients.

2. From 2009, to reduce the costs involved in the renegotiations done by the account managers, a computer program was launched that renegotiated automatically the debt of 30,000 customers each month, incorporating abusive interests unilaterally without the need of personal or telephonic contact with the customers. This way, it modified its customers' default, who ignored what happened to their account since they were never consulted whether they needed to renegotiate the debt.

With both practices, La Polar converted a delinquent customer balance into profits. For this to happen, the entire outstanding balance is renegotiated (interests, arrears, collection expenses, etc.) and then it is posted as if the customer had paid it in exchange for a new and higher credit, registering a profit for the increase of the balance that the customer will have to pay in the future. Thus, for example, customers who bought the equivalent to 100 euros, after several unilateral renegotiations were left owing over 2,000 euros. From the 1.2 million customers of La Polar, 418,000 were victims of this crime.

With the practices described, the company, which sold on credit to customers with a low-credit profile to contain the fall on sales due to the crisis, transformed a negative EBITDA into profits once the interests from the renegotiations were incorporated. In total, it is estimated that the profits were fraudulently increased by 582 million euros.

Figure 10.9 shows how the company compensated the decline in sales with the increase of financial income, which came from 80% of the fraudulent renegotiations of delinquent balances.

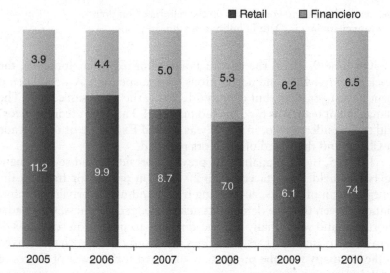

FIGURE 10.9 Evolution of the retail (sales) income and the financial income of La Polar between 2005 and 2010
Source: La Polar, Report 2011. Data in billion of Chilean Pesos.

With these manipulations, the company got the share price to be very favorable. During those years, the president of the company, along

(Continued)

with several directors and managers constituted several companies that bought shares of La Polar and sold them collecting substantial profits. In doing so through companies, it wasn't registered that they were the ones who controlled the company's shares.

To visualize the impact of the manipulation in the accounts, see Figure 10.10. In 2011, once the fictitious customer balances were cancelled and the equity was adjusted, the company was left with a negative equity. Therefore, the manipulation concealed that the company was registering losses and that it was bankrupt.

	2008	2009	2010	2011
Total assets	699	804	910	334
Equity	230	332	344	−228
Liabilities	469	472	566	562
Total Equity + Liabilities	699	804	910	334

FIGURE 10.10   Evolution of the summarized balance of La Polar from 2008 to 2011
Source: Authors own work based on the reports of La Polar (www.nuevapolar.cl). Data in billions of Chilean pesos.

On June 9, 2011, the day La Polar admitted its malpractice, the stock price fell 42% and negotiations were suspended. A week later, it went back to trading, but on July 21, 2011, the price sank 86%. The management team was fired (including the CIO and the credit director) and the president (who, in 2009, was elected Executive of the Decade in Chile), and the board of directors resigned.

In 2015, the trial against the previous president and several managers was held. They faced up to 20 years in prison for fraud in the renegotiation of credits, accounting fraud, and use of privileged information. Given that the defendants acknowledged the facts, they had a short trial and were finally sentenced merely to probation sentences of between two and five years, with fines for the amount they had received in the company plus the profits they obtained for the sale of shares of La Polar.

In this case, the evolution of customer balances, financial income, and delinquency, compared to data from the competition, were the warning signs that some detected.

10.10   SYNTHETIC INDEX TO DETECT MANIPULATING COMPANIES

Z indexes are also used to detect companies with a high probability of having manipulated the accounts. The first use of this technique was done by Beneish (1999). Next, we show an index calculated from a sample of 63 companies, among which were 35 manipulating companies and 28 nonmanipulating (Vladu, Amat, and Cuzdrorien, 2016).

Through the discriminant analysis, four ratios were identified that allow detecting companies with a higher probability of having manipulated their accounts.

Ratio 1: Index of customers to sales.

$$(\text{Accounts receivable}_n/\text{Sales}_n)/(\text{Accounts receivable}_{n-1}/\text{Sales}_{n-1})$$

When it increases it is a sign of possible manipulation.

Ratio 2: Index of inventory to cost of sales.

$$(\text{Inventory}_n/\text{Cost of sales}_n)/(\text{Inventory}_{n-1}/\text{Cost of sales}_{n-1})$$

When it increases it is a sign of possible manipulation.

Ratio 3: Index of depreciations compared to property, plant, and equipment

$$(\text{Amortiz}_n/\text{Property, plant, and equipment}_n)/$$

$$(\text{Amortiz}_{n-1}/\text{Property, plant, and equipment}_{n-1})$$

When it decreases it is a sign of possible manipulation.

Ratio 4: Index of debt to assets.

$$(\text{Current liabilities}_n/\text{Assets}_n)/(\text{Current liabilities}_{n-1}/\text{Assets}_{n-1})$$

When it increases it is a sign of possible manipulation.

The formula is the following:

$$Z = -4.5 + (0.03 \times R1) + (0.15 \times R2) - (0.17 \times R3) + (4.23 \times R4)$$

And it is analyzed considering that:

- Value greater than +0.20: High probability that the company manipulates accounts.
- Value between −0.24 and +0.20: Intermediate zone where there is no sign of manipulation or nonmanipulation.
- Value below −0.24: High probability that the company doesn't manipulate accounts.

EXAMPLE: USING THE Z-SCORE TO DETECT ACCOUNT MANIPULATIONS

In Figure 10.11 we can see an application of the last Z-Score to detect if a company has manipulated the accounts.

Detecting Account Manipulation (2009)			
	Company X	Average Manipulators	Average Non Manipulators
Receivable Index	0.68	1.39	1.34
Inventories Index	0.00	1.23	1.15
Depreciation Index	7.38	1.03	1.08
Leverage Index	0.95	1.1	1
Z Score Vladu, Amat and Cuzdrioream	−1.73	0.2	−0.24

Detecting Account Manipulation (2013)			
	Company X	Average Manipulators	Average Non Manipulators
Receivable Index	1.80	1.39	1.34
Inventories Index	0.34	1.23	1.15
Depreciation Index	6.46	1.03	1.08
Leverage Index	1.34	1.1	1
Z Score Vladu, Amat and Cuzdrioream	0.18	0.2	−0.24

FIGURE 10.11 Applying the Z-Score to detect account manipulations in a company in the year 2009 and 2013

In Figure 10.11 we observe that in 2009 company X had a low probability of being a manipulator because the value of its Z-score was −1.73 and this value was closer to the value of non-manipulators (−0.24). In 2013, the situation changed because the value of the Z-score for company X was 0.18 and this was a value closer to the value for manipulators (0.2).

Practical Case of Using an Audit Report to Detect Accounting Fraud

This case has the objective of illustrating how the reading of the audit reports provides very useful information to better understand the real situation of the company.

This is a group of companies that produce components to several industrial sectors. It is a real case, although the company's name has been modified. Following the latest balance sheet and income statement, we also see three ratios (liquidity, debt, and profitability). See Figures 10.12, 10.13, and 10.14.

	Year 0
Intangible fixed assets	1,478
Tangible fixed assets	2,735
Own shares	835
Total noncurrent assets	**5,048**
Inventory	208
Debtors	4,709
Treasury	377
Current assets	**5,294**
Assets	**10,342**
Equity	**2,097**
Noncurrent liabilities	**4,933**
Debts with credit institutions	1,435
Trade creditors	1,816
Provisions	61
Current liabilities	**3,312**
Liabilities and equity	**10,342**

FIGURE 10.12 Consolidated balance sheet of the Group of Industrial Services for year 0 (data in thousands of euros)

(Continued)

	Year 0
Sales	13,906
Operating expenses	−12,604
Operating result (EBIT)	**1,302**
Financial expenses	−699
Results before taxes (RBT)	**603**
Income tax	−275
Net profit	**328**

FIGURE 10.13 Consolidated income statement of the Group of Industrial Services (data in thousands of euros)

Ratios	Year 0
Liquidity Current assets/Current liabilities	1.6
Indebtedness Liabilities/Assets	0.8
ROE Net profit/Equity	0.15

FIGURE 10.14 Ratios of the Group of Industrial Services

The previous ratios show a liquidity that seems to be sufficient (since the current assets far exceed current liabilities, the indebtedness is high).

The audit report of year 1 includes the following exceptions:

1. *The Group keeps included in the item Current Assets Debtors accounts receivable with associates amounting to a total of 1,604 thousand euros and without giving enough information to be able to evaluate its remnant.*
2. *The company maintains its own shares valued at 835 thousand euros. The adjustments of these shares to their theoretical book value would result in a capital loss of the same amount.*
3. *The Group has resolved a contract with a supplier in advance, as a result of which it would have to provide 79 thousand euros in compensation.*

The report includes the following final opinion: "In our opinion, given the importance of the qualifications described, the consolidated annual accounts of the attached year don't express the true image of the equity and the financial situation of Industrial Services and Subsidiaries at December 31st of year 0 and the result of its operations during the annual exercise ended on that date, according to the generally accepted accounting principles and standards."

In view of the previous information, the Group of Industrial Services should recalculate the annual accounts and the ratios of liquidity, indebtedness, and profitability when incorporating the qualifications included in the audit report.

Proposed Solution

According to the exceptions included in the auditors' report, the following adjustments should be made (see Figures 10.15, 10.16 and 10.17).

	Year 0	Adjustments	Year 0 Adjusted
Intangible fixed assets	1,478		1,478
Tangible fixed assets	2,735		2,735
Own shares	835	−835	0
Total noncurrent assets	**5,048**		**4,213**
Inventory	208		208
Debtors	4,709	−1,604	3,105
Treasury	377		377
Current assets	**5,294**		**3,690**
Assets	**10,342**		**7,903**
Equity	**2,097**	−1,604 −835 −79	**−421**
Noncurrent liabilities	**4,933**		**4,933**
Debts with credit institutions	1,435		1,435
Trade creditors	1,816		1,816
Provisions	61	+79	140
Current liabilities	**3,312**		**3,391**
Liabilities and equity	**10,342**		**7,903**

FIGURE 10.15 Consolidated balance sheet of the Group of Industrial Services for year 0 (data in thousands of euros)

(Continued)

	Year 0	Adjustments	Year 0 Adjusted
Sales	13,906		13,906
Operating expenses	−12,604		−12,604
Provisions and impairments		−1,604 −835 −79	−2,518
Earnings Before Interest and Taxes (EBIT)	**1,302**		**−2,026**
Financial expenses	−699		−699
Earnings Before Tax (EBT)	**603**		**−2,725**
Income tax	−275		−275
Net profit	**328**		**−3,000**

FIGURE 10.16 Consolidated income statements of the Group Industrial Services (data in thousands of euros)

According to the previous adjustment, the ratios would be as follows.

Ratios	Year 0 Without Adjustments	Year 0 With Adjustments
Liquidity Current assets/Current liabilities	1.6	1.08
Indebtedness Liabilities/Assets	0.8	1.05
Profitability Net profit/Equity	0.15	Negative

FIGURE 10.17 Ratios of the Group of Industrial Services

From the above it follows that if we consider the qualifications included in the auditors' report, this company has a much lower liquidity (it goes from 1.6 to 1.08), negative equity (the debts exceed the assets), and negative returns.

Key Topics of the Chapter

Many warning signals can be found in the accounts that inform auditors of possible accounting manipulations. Among the main warning signals, we mention the following.

- Exceptions in the audit report, or negative or denied opinion.
- Balance sheet: off-balance-sheet operations, operating leases that are actually acquisitions, significant variations in terms, discrepancies between the variations of customers, inventory or suppliers, in relation to the evolution of the sales or purchases.
- Income statement: inconsistency between sales and operational indicators, changes in the expense capitalization policy, very conservative or very optimistic estimates, changes in the revenue recognition policy, losses charged to reserves, and so on.
- Cash flow statement: differences between the cash flow (net profit plus depreciation) and the cash generated by operations.
- Statement of changes in equity: adjustments for changes in criterion or errors.
- Notes (lack of consolidation of subsidiaries, off-balance sheet operations, transactions without economic sense).
- Ratios that anticipate frauds: reduction in profitability and margin; deterioration of liquidity and debts, and so on.
- Unjustified variations in accounts.
- Ratios that indicate that a fraud may have occurred: term ratios and turnovers.
- Synthetic index to detect manipulations.

REFERENCES

Altman, E. (1968). Financial ratios, discriminant analysis and the prediction of corporate bankruptcy, *Journal of Finance* 23 (4).
Amat, O., Antón, M., and Manini, R. (2016). Credit concessions through credit scoring. Analysis and application proposal. *Intangible Capital* (December).
Baires, R., Sullivan, J., and Chávez, A. (2011). *La Polar: Historia de una gran estafa*, CIPER. http://ciperchile.cl/wp-content/uploads/LT-POLAR-RB-ACH-FINAL_2.pdf.
Beasley, S.M., Carcello, J., and Hermanson, D.R. (2000). *Fraudulent financial reporting: 1987–1997: An analysis of US Public Companies*. Research Report. Committee of Sponsoring Organizations.
Beneish, M.D. (1999). Incentives and penalties related to earnings overstatements that violate GAAP. *The Accounting Review* 74 (4): 425–457.
Calderon, T.G., and Green, B.P. (1994). Signaling fraud by using analytical procedures. *Ohio CPA Journal* 53 (2): 27–38.
Davia, H.R., Coggins, P.C., Wideman, J.E., and Kastantin, I.T. (2000). *Accountant's guide to fraud detection and control*. New York: Wiley.

Du Toit, E. (2008). Characteristics of companies with a higher risk of financial statement fraud: A survey of the literature. Working Paper. Department of Financial Management. University of Pretoria, South Africa. http://www.repository .up.ac.za/bitstream/handle/2263/9141/DuToit_Characteristics(2008).pdf? sequence=1

Eusebio, N. (2016). How to detect account manipulation. *Revista de Contabilidad y Dirección* (23): 153–176.

Kaminski, K.A., Wetzel, T.S., and Guan L. (2004). Can financial ratios detect fraudulent financial reporting? *Managerial Auditing Journal* 19 (1): 15–28.

Ketz, J.E. (2003). *Hidden Financial Risk: Understanding Off-Balance Sheet Financing*. Hoboken, NJ: Wiley.

Krambia-Kapardis, M. (2002). A fraud detection model: A must for auditors. *Journal of Financial Regulation and Compliance* 10 (3): 266–278.

Lee, T.A., Ingram, R.W., and Howard, T.P. (1999). The difference between earnings and operating cash flow as an indicator of financial reporting fraud. *Contemporary Accounting Research* 16 (4): 749–786.

Lendez, A.M., and Korevec, U. (1999). How to prevent and detect financial statement fraud. *The Journal of Corporate Accounting & Finance* 11 (1): 47–54.

Mulford, C.W., and Comiskey, E.E. (2002). *The Financial Numbers Game. Detecting Creative Accounting Practices*. New York/Wiley.

Mulford, C.W., and Comiskey, E.E. (2005). *Creative Cash Flow Reporting*. New York: Wiley.

Özcan, A. (2016). Firm characteristics and accounting fraud: A multivariate approach. *Journal of Accounting, Finance and Auditing Studies* 2 (2): 128–144.

Persons, O.S. (1995). Using financial statement data to identify factors associated with fraudulent financial reporting. *Journal of Applied Business Research*. 11 (3): 38–47.

Rezaee, Z. (2002). *Financial Statement Fraud: Prevention and Detection*. New York: Wiley.

Schilit, H.M. (1993). *Financial Shenanigans: How to Detect Accounting Gimmicks and Fraud in Financial Reports*. New York: McGraw-Hill.

Sloan, R.G. (1996). Do stock prices fully reflect information in accruals and cash flows about future earnings? *The Accounting Review* (3): 289–315.

Spathis, C., Doumpos, M., and Zopoundinis, C. (2002). Detecting falsified financial statements: A comparative study using multicriteria analysis and multivariate statistical techniques. *The European Accounting Review* 11 (3): 509–535.

Vladu, A.B, Amat, O., and Cuzdrorien, D.D. (2016). Truthfulness in accounting: How to discriminate accounting manipulators from non-manipulators, *Journal of Business Ethics* 140 (4): 633–648.

Wharton. (2011). El escándalo contable de La Polar provoca escalofríos en Chile. http://www.knowledgeatwharton.com.es/article/el-escandalo-contable-de-la-polar-provoca-escalofrios-en-chile/.

CHAPTER **11**

Some Suggestions to Improve the Current Situation

Corruption, embezzlement, fraud, these are all characteristics which exist everywhere. It is regrettably the way human nature functions, whether we like it or not. What successful economies do is keep it to a minimum. No one has ever eliminated any of that stuff.

—Alan Greenspan (former president of the
US Federal Reserve, 2007)

As we have been seeing throughout the book, accounting fraud is lethal for companies and those who have trust in them. It damages trust in the economic system of a country, as well as its companies and institutions. It also affects negatively the accounting and auditing profession. Therefore, it is necessary to fight fraud with all possible weapons.

In this chapter we propose measures that could reduce deceits and improve the reliability of the companies' financial information. As shown in Figure 11.1, and remembering the concept of the door to fraud, these measures are proposed to act against the four big factors that explain the occurrence of frauds.

11.1 REINFORCE VALUES AND INSTITUTE ETHICAL CODES

Fraud and deceit are inherent to the human condition. It isn't realistic to imagine a world without fraud. However, as the populations' values improve, frauds will reduce. Therefore, a key element in the fight against accounting manipulations is to influence the ethical basis and values.

Values are beliefs that guide people's conduct. Although we talk about lack of values, the problem is that bad values are gaining ground each day. Good values like integrity, honesty, loyalty, social responsibility, humility, justice, and a culture of effort are surpassed by the culture of greed, perverse incentive systems, insensibility, or lack of ethics. The bad example given by

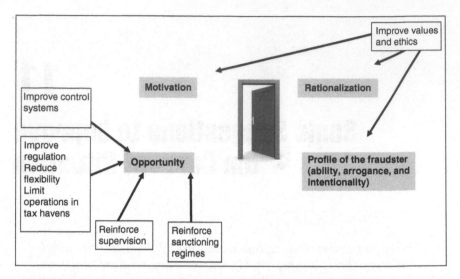

FIGURE 11.1   The door to fraud and several measures to reduce frauds

too many leaders and rulers, and our social tolerance of fraud, aggravate the situation. All of this contributes to more collective dehumanization and this also affects many companies, where with each passing day the crisis of values becomes more evident.

However, multiple studies show that the companies that are managed with good values do much better and live longer. For example, Webley and More (2003) highlight that companies that implement ethics codes are 50% more profitable than those who don't. Companies with good values keep their customers, employees, and other related parties more satisfied, which results in better results. As it has often been show, the best business it to be honest.

Let's remember some of the most relevant values.

Teamwork

Commitment to people; employees are not mere instruments for share-holders to get rich. This implies teamwork, dialogue, empathy, fairness, humility, and closeness. Values related to how things are done are also key. For example, the passion for work well done and customer satisfaction are essential, as is the ability to adapt to the accelerated changes of the market.

Social Responsibility

Another value to highlight is social responsibility, since it is common among successful companies to revert to the society a part of the profits obtained and to be actively concerned about the environment.

Incentives and Values

Many cases of success transmit that values are more important than immediate economic profit; and they show it with incentive systems that are aligned with values. That is to say, they are not perverse remuneration systems that award results based on the exploitation of employees or customer, and that usually end in big scandals.

In short, nowadays values can be sources of competitive advantages since they are increasingly appreciated by customers, employees and other concerned parties. And the challenge is to have solid values that endure over time, even if there are changes in the composition of the team. In this way, companies that have good and solid values get more satisfaction, commitment, and profitability. In addition, they reduce the probability of frauds.

It is necessary to influence the ethical bases of the population and for this, the role of the education and values transmitted by families and the media is essential.

About education, often business schools are criticized. For example, in 2005, *The Wall Street Journal* published the results of a survey that showed that a large part of the big financial scandals had been carried out by graduates of the best business schools. In its conclusions, it pointed out as causes the obsession for making money regardless of ethical principles.

11.2 IMPROVE CONTROL SYSTEMS IN ORGANIZATIONS

But we can't reform ourselves by only improving values and ethical standards. In the United States, criminologists use the rule 10–80–10 (unknown origin) that consists in considering that 10% of the population will never commit frauds, whether by religious, moral, or other convictions. Another 10% will try to commit fraud, even when it is very difficult to do. Finally, the remaining 80% of the population will not commit fraud if the regulation and control systems make it difficult, and the punishments are exemplary. Therefore, it is about acting and thinking about 80% of the population, using good legislation and a justice system that is fast and exemplary.

Since it is impossible to completely eradicate fraud, we must reduce opportunities for them to occur. Remember, 47% of frauds occur in companies with deficient control systems (KPMG, 2013). Measures such as the following that improve the internal control of companies have proven to be very effective.

- Reinforce internal audit.
- Make surprise audits.
- Create an audit committee with independent and competent people, and a crime prevention committee. Currently, companies that aren't authorized to present abbreviated profit and loss accounts are obliged

to institute these committees if they want to meet one of the conditions established for the exemption from criminal liability of the legal entity (Riera and Ruano, 2016).

- Provide to the shareholders the minutes of the Audit Committee meetings.
- Members of the Audit Committee shouldn't participate in the variable retribution programs.
- Auditors attendance to the annual general meetings to answer questions directly to the shareholders.
- Introduce an anonymous reporting hotline.
- Active participation of the members of the board on the control mechanisms.
- Independent people with extensive knowledge in accounting on the board of directors. Boards of directors that are more independent are more likely to introduce anonymous reporting channels, which have been proven to be very useful to discover frauds (Johansson and Carey 2016).
- Periodic analysis of the areas susceptible to frauds.
- Periodic programs of fraud prevention.

Let's see some examples of measures that have gotten good results.

The Department of Internal Audit at Worldcom

The accounting fraud at WorldCom, which broke out in 2002, was one of the biggest scandals to ever occur after the burst of the internet bubble of the year 2000. The manipulation consisted in overvaluing assets in over $11 million through the fraudulent capitalization of expenses and the nonaccounting of other expenses. Fictitious income was also accounted for. Those responsible were the CFO and the controller who obeyed the instructions of President Bernie Ebbers. The department of internal audit discovered the fraud. Shortly after, the company went bankrupt, destroying 30,000 jobs and causing $180 million losses to shareholders.

The president, the man responsible, was sentenced to 25 years in prison for fraud and for falsifying financial records. The CFO was dismissed and the controller resigned. Shortly after this scandal, the US Congress approved the Sarbanes–Oxley Act, which was the biggest reform in the commercial law produced since 1930. The name of this Act honors two of its main promoters: Senator Paul Sarbanes and the Representative Michael Oxley.

Anonymous Reporting Hotline at Waste Management

In 1998, this company posted $1.7 million in fictitious profits. The manipulation, which consisted in increasing the term of depreciation of its buildings and machinery, was discovered when there was a change in president and the management team. The previous management and the auditors had signed a contract to keep the fraud for five years. Therefore, the SEC fined the auditor $7 million and the shareholders got the company to pay them compensation of $457 million.

After the scandal, the company started a hotline where employees could anonymously report dishonest behaviors.

Eric Ben-Artzi, Deusche Bank Employee Who Reported Accounting Frauds Related to Derivatives

At the end of 2016, the Deutsche Bank was in a very difficult situation. The media overflowed with news about the banks' need for capital and a possible bailout by Germany.

The share price of the bank reached $153.55 on April 30, 2007, and sunk to $13.09 on September 30, 2016 (see Figure 11.2).

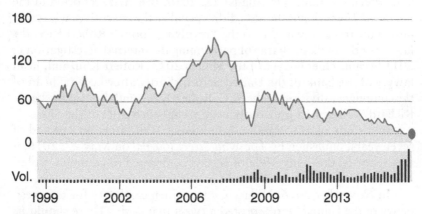

FIGURE 11.2 The Price of Deutsche Bank AG between 1999 and October 6, 2016

The bank's problems started to come to light due to the complaints by Eric Ben-Artzi, a doctor in mathematics, who went to work in the American subsidiary of Deustche Bank in 2010. After a while, he started to notice that something wasn't done correctly in the bank. Specifically,

(Continued)

he detected accounting practices that inflated its portfolio of credit derivatives (valued at $120 million) and, simultaneously, losses were concealed. This was the biggest portfolio the companies that operated in Wall Street had. These manipulations were done due to the crash of 2008. Ben-Artzi informed a lawyer at the bank about his findings, Robert Rice. Rice told him not to divulge the problem. Ben-Artzi disagreed and was fired for it, ruining his career on Wall Street.

He didn't give up. Shortly after, in 2011, Ben-Artzi and two other colleagues decided to go one step further and reported the frauds to the Securities and Exchange Commission (SEC). After a long process, the SEC imposed a fine of 55 million euros to the company, after estimating they had hidden about $12 million in losses.

The SEC wanted to reward his information with $8.5 million (half of the 15% of the fine imposed on Deutsche Bank), but Ben-Artzi rejected it, since he only wanted those responsible for the fraud to pay for it and he didn't want to receive money that was actually being paid by the shareholders of the Deutsche Bank. In addition, he reported that the SEC should have fined the executives who committed the fraud (who, in addition, had received multimillion-dollar bonuses) and not the bank since in the end those who paid for it were the shareholders, who weren't at fault. On August 18, 2016, Ben-Artzi reported in the *Financial Times* that if the SEC didn't penalize the executives who committed the fraud, it was due to the "revolving doors": Robert Rice, the lawyer of the bank in charge of performing the internal investigation in 2011 became chief lawyer of the SEC in 2013. Robert Khuzami, head lawyer of the bank in the United States, shortly after became head of the compliance division of the SEC. Robert Khuzami's boss at the bank, Richard Walker, had previously been compliance chief at the SEC.

In a study of 156 frauds committed at Wall Street in a period of seven years, published by *The Wall Street Journal* on May 27, 2016, it was reported that only 19% of frauds committed in companies punished the people who committed it.

In November 2016, Hillary Clinton, then candidate for the presidency of the United States, posted a tweet that said: "There should be no bank too big to fail and no individual too big to jail."

Some Lessons from the Case

- It is a bad practice not allowing employees to disagree and not analyzing well the reasons for the discrepancies and how to correct the mistakes; the employees can also divulge it elsewhere.

- When punishing for fraud, you have to make sure to penalize those who commit it. Shareholders may not always be guilty of what the managers of their companies do.
- Employees who report frauds don't always do it for money; they may do it for ethical reasons and a sense of justice.
- The existence of complaint channels enables frauds to be discovered.

11.3 IMPROVE REGULATION

According to the rule 10–80–10 mentioned in the previous section, regulation and justice are key to reduce frauds. If we want to reduce accounting frauds, it is indispensable to improve the regulations. In this sense, several measures could be beneficial:

1. **Reduce the flexibility of the accounting standards.**

   As has been shown, one of the big problems with the standards is that almost all elements of the balance sheet and income statement have different alternatives regarding their accounting, or they require estimates (which involve a high dose of subjectivity) to do the valuation. Therefore:
   - To reduce the opportunities that allow doing legal accounting manipulations, the alternatives should be eliminated. In this way, interested postings that lead to legal manipulations would be avoided. For example, research and development in many countries can be considered an expense or an asset. As there may be companies interested in increasing the profit (they will consider R&D as an asset, in countries where this is possible) or reducing the profit (they will consider R+D as an expense). What is proposed is giving R&D a single possible treatment through which the possibility to choose the most advantageous alternative will be eliminated. This is the case with US GAAP where R&D is an expense.
   - The field of estimates should also be reduced. An example would be the impairment of customers that currently doesn't have a concrete accounting regulation. What could be done, since it already exists in taxation, is setting the impairment permanently depending on the time elapsed since the customer had to be charged. For example, after six months since the maturity it could be deteriorated 25%, after 12 months 50%, after 18 months 75%, and after two years it deteriorates 100%.

These measures could help the accounting report facts and not conjectures about the future of the company.

2. **Limit operations with tax havens.**

We have recalled several examples where accounting frauds were done through subsidiaries in tax havens. On the other hand, the European Commission reported in 2016 that between tax engineering and fraud, one billion euros a year is lost in the European Union. As a consequence, the commission recommends member states to introduce in their tax regime an *anti-abuse clause* to prevent multinationals taking advantage of the differences between countries to avoid paying taxes.

If you want to reduce the opportunities for accounting fraud you have to limit operations with tax havens. But, in addition, it would be convenient that at an international scale and, especially, in the EU, taxation be harmonized and the eternal pending issue of tax havens solved once and for all.

Given that it isn't easy to improve the current fiscal framework, it would be desirable for multinationals that practice aggressive fiscal strategies to adopt a more socially responsible attitude and pay income taxes in countries where they generate wealth.

3. **Reduce mandatory information.**

Another problem is the excess of information. As it is often said: The best way to not inform is to provide an excess of information. Lev (2016) provides evidence that if companies suppress trimestral reports, 33% of the surveyed CFOs consider that no information useful for investors is lost, and 80% considers that the savings in information production costs is worth it. Therefore, we propose reducing the mandatory information with the aim of focusing on the key aspects of the business that allow users to diagnose the current situation and the company's future perspectives.

11.4 REINFORCE SUPERVISION

The supervisory institutions have also been questioned when accounting frauds occur for not having acted of time. Therefore, there are measures that can contribute to improve its efficiency in fraud prevention, such as:

- These institutions should have more resources and personnel.
- They shouldn't authorize specific treatments outside of accounting regulations.
- Start an anonymous complaint channel in the supervisory institution.

THE ANONYMOUS COMPLAINT CHANNEL OF THE SEC

The start of this channel for anonymous complaints is having a lot of success in the several countries that have launched it. For example, in the United States, the SEC started one in 2011 and received 334 anonymous complaints that year. Since then, complaints have been increasing steadily. In 2015, for example, it already received 3,923. The tipoffs related to accounting frauds are the most frequent and represent 18% of the total. The second most frequent type of complaints is related to cases of usage of privileged information (16% of the total).

The SEC awards complainants with a part of the sanction that it imposes to the offenders, and in 2015 paid $38 million to whistleblowers.

11.5 REINFORCE THE SANCTIONING REGIME

Countries that have tougher sanctions against fraud, with fast judicial systems that enforce the sentences applied, usually have less fraud. As proven by the Nobel laureate Gary Becker (1974), tough legislation doesn't completely eliminate fraud, but it greatly discourages it. In this sense we recall that in mid-twentieth century, the United States was one of the most corrupt countries in the world. In a few years they managed to greatly reduce corruption through a quick legal system and tougher sanctions.

Without a doubt, if the legal system in a country is slow, the fines very low, and they aren't obeyed, it is a breeding ground for frauds to increase.

In Anglo–Saxon countries, fines for economic frauds (including accounting frauds) are very tough and it is frequent for hundreds-of-million- or even billion-dollar fines to be imposed. These are sanctions that have an important deterrent function. However, in other countries, it is very common for sanctions for economic crimes to be so small that they allow frauds to be very cheap for those who commit them.

For example, in Spain the CNMV (the Spanish stock exchange supervisor) imposed 77 fines in 2014 for a total amount of 17 million euros; in 2015 there were 90 fines for a total value of 20 million euros. It is similar in volume to that of the French stock exchange supervisor (AFM), that in 2014 imposed 79 economic sanctions for a total amount of 32 million euros. On the other hand, the FSA (British supervisor) imposed 41 sanctions in 2014, for a total amount of 1,984 million euros, and the American SEC, that same year, imposed 755 sanctions for a total amount of 4,100 million euros.

11.6   THE CHALLENGE OF PROVIDING RELEVANT INFORMATION FOR DECISION-MAKING

In previous sections we have defended the argument that accounting regulations should eliminate its flexibility to be as objective as possible. This proposal has the problem that it could produce information that is more objective but more irrelevant. For example, valuing a property acquired 30 years ago using the acquisition price provides an objective data but very far from its current value.

At this point, we can't forget the fundamental aim of accounting: to provide information that is relevant for decision-making.

Both aims (objectivity and relevance) can often be incompatible since objectivity requires giving priority to the acquisition price, while relevance implies giving priority to the market value.

For this, we formulate another proposal with the aim of also having information that is relevant and useful for decision-making. This is about the companies preparing the annual accounts clearly separating two types of information:

1. On one hand, annual accounts using rigid accounting standards and without room for legal accounting manipulations. The valuation of assets and expenses should be based on the acquisition price (acquisition or market, the lowest) and thus the accounts would be formulated more objectively, although it is irrelevant information with certain assets (such as real estate or intangibles).
2. Additionally, they could present accounts with realistic values based on the market price, especially in the case of real estate and intangibles (brands, patents, distribution network, and so on). This information would be less objective but would provide more relevant data for decision-making. Also, information based on market value should be incorporated as supplementary indicators that add value to the company, but is difficult to quantify in monetary units. We are talking about, for example, information about key success factors like customer satisfaction, quality of product and service, innovation, or employee satisfaction (see Lev, 2016).

Given the degree of subjectivity that involves, in many cases, the use of market price, it should be accompanied by the favorable opinion of an independent expert.[1] This way, it is possible to improve the reliability of the information provided.

---

[1]There are international precedents for this type of assessment. For example, in the Andorra GAAP, Law 30/2007 of December 20, is included the revalued value, which "is an assets' fair value at the moment of is revaluation, minus the accumulated

In the case of intangibles, especially those where there isn't an active market that enables quantifying the fair value in a verifiable way, caution is recommended when doing the valuation. Therefore, it must be taken into consideration that the auditor gives his agreement to the figures mentioned in the report. Thus, though there is an assessment done by an expert, the auditor has to consider if he considers reasonable the valuation systems used and their conclusions.

According to this proposal, the accounts would have two additional columns. One column with the adjustments proposed and the other column with the resulting data.

The proposal to formulate two types of accounts has a precedent in the United States with the so-called Non-US GAAP Earnings (profits that don't follow the US Generally Accepted Accounting Principles). In the United States, companies are obliged to follow the accounting standards (US GAAP) but they are allowed to complement this information with data prepared without these rules, called the Non-US GAAP. This supplementary information includes data of incomes and profits without including expenses that aren't paid (like depreciations, impairments or restructuring provisions) and adding that they have been charged but are accrued in subsequent years.

Figure 11.3 shows the two types of data as provided by Microsoft.

Next, we see a real case of a company where the accounting information could improve substantially if this proposal was applied.

	Income	Operating profit	Net profit
Accounts based on the US GAAP	**+20,614**	**+3,080**	**+3,122**
Impact of depreciation, impairments and provisions for restructuring	+2,028	+2,028	+1,467
Impact of deferred income	—	+1,110	+895
Accounts not based on the US GAAP	**+22,642**	**+6,218**	**+5,484**

FIGURE 11.3 Microsoft's revenues and profits with accounting principles and complemented accounts that include adjustments not based on the accounting principles (data in millions of dollars)
Source: Microsoft Accounts of 2016 (First Quarter) (www.microsoft.com).

---

depreciation and the subsequent accumulated impairment losses. Every revaluation must be justified by an appraisal from an independent expert, of proven technical solvency." At the Spanish level, the specific legislation of insurance entities through its supervisory body, the General Directorate of Insurance and Pensions, establishes the assessment criteria for real estate and certain real rights for the purpose of covering technical provisions. In this sense, it manifests the Order EHA/3011/2007, of October 4 that modifies it.

REAL CASE OF A COMPANY WITH SIGNIFICANT CAPITAL GAINS NOT INCLUDED IN THE ACCOUNTING

It is a company that has property valued at an acquisition price minus depreciation (2 million euros) that is much lower than its fair value of 56 million euros. Its other intangibles don't have any book value according to current regulations, despite the fact, according to market prices, its value is estimated in 182 million euros.

In the notes, it could be included in the following information:

In the company's assets, which include properties with a book value of 2 million euros. According to the appraisal done by XX, its fair value is estimated in 56 million euros.

The company owns several brands that have a book value of zero for being totally amortized. According to the appraisal done by WW, its fair value is estimated in 62 million euros.

The entity has several intangible assets that, according to current legislation, have a book value of zero. However, according to the appraisal done by YY, its fair value is estimated at 182 million euros.

The recognition of the indicated capital gains implies that the company's equity should increase in 298 million euros.

Next, we see the company's adjusted balance sheet, once the proposed adjustments are incorporated:

	Balance Sheet Prepared with Objectivity	Adjustments	Balance Sheet that Provides Relevant Information for Decision-Making
Noncurrent assets	371	+54 +62 +182	669
Current assets	82		82
Total assets	453	+298	751
Equity	−59	+54 +62 +182	239
Non-current liabilities	223		223
Current liabilities	289		289
Total equity plus liabilities	453	+298	751

Once the adjustments have been made, the increase in the value of the assets explains that the net equity has a positive value, which is closer to the company's reality.

The proposals formulated in this chapter may be ambitious, but if regulators, managers, board of directors, accountants, analysts, and other agents don't follow this track, and fast, we will continue disappointing users and we will lose a good opportunity to get the financial information to be reliable and useful for decision-making.

Key Topics of the Chapter

Given the lethal effects of accounting frauds, there is no need to spare measures to reduce the magnitude of the problem. There are many initiatives that can be implemented to reduce accounting manipulations.

- Reinforce values and ethical standards.
- Implement codes of conduct.
- Improve control systems in the company.
- Implement a channel of anonymous complaints in the companies and the supervisory entities.
- Improve regulation.
- Implement a regime of dissuasive sanctions in case of frauds and prompt justice.
- To avoid legal manipulations in the financial information, it should be based on objective rules (for example, acquisition price). But in order to have useful information for decision-making, it would be necessary to incorporate complementary information that is closer to reality (based on market price).

REFERENCES

Amat, O. (2014). Las empresas con buenos valores van mejor. *La Vanguardia* (9 November).

Amat, O., and Oliveras, E. (2004): Propuestas para combatir la contabilidad creativa, *Universia Business Review* (1): 10–17.

Becker, G.S., and Landes, W.M. (1974). *Essays in the Economics of Crime and Punishment.* Cambridge, MA: NBER.

Ben-Artzi, E. (2016). We must protect shareholders from executive wrongdoing. *Financial Times* (18 August).

Dechow, P., and Skinner, D.J. (2000). Earnings management: Reconciling the views of accounting, academics, practitioners, and regulators. *Accounting Horizons* 14 (2): 235–250.

Johansson, E., and Carey, P. (2016). Detecting fraud: The role of the anonymous reporting channel. *Journal of Business Ethics* 139 (2): 391–409.

Johnson, D. (2015). *Ethics at Work*. London: Institute of Business Ethics.

KPMG. (2013). *A survey of fraud, bribery and corruption in Australia & New Zealand* 2012.

Lev, B. (2016). *The End of Accounting and the Path Forward for Investors and Managers*. Hoboken, NJ: Wiley.

Riera, J., and Ruano, P. (2016). Diseño del sistema organizativo y de control interno para la prevención y detección del fraude. *Revista de Contabilidad y Dirección* (23): 41–60.

Sherwood, B. (2010). *The Survivors Club: The Secrets and Science that Could Save Your Life*. Grand Central Publishing: New York.

Tipgos, M.A. (2002). Why management fraud is unstoppable. *The CPA Journa.* 72 (12): 34–41.

Webley, S., and More, E. (2003). *Does Business Ethics Pay? Ethics and Financial Performance*. London: Institute of Business Ethics.

Epilogue

Fraud—the need to exaggerate achievements and hide failures—is inherent to human nature and not many people escape this type of temptations.

Therefore, a good way to minimize the risks of manipulation is to always analyze the accounts with a hint of skepticism that helps us not to overlook warning signs.

Of all the warning signs shown in previous chapters, we can propose the following 10 as the most important ones:

1. Deficient control systems.
2. Absence of complaints channels.
3. Excessively complex corporate structure and subsidiaries in tax havens.
4. Speculative operations with financial derivatives that are difficult to understand.
5. Managers with extravagant lifestyles and many luxuries.
6. Managers with conflict of interests in relation to customers, suppliers, bank . . .
7. Qualifications in the audit report.
8. Increase of debts.
9. Discrepancies between sales, profits, customer balances, and inventory.
10. Discrepancies between the profit generated and the cash.

The presence of warning signs doesn't necessarily imply that there is fraud, but it informs us that extreme precautions must be taken.

Criminal Responsibility of Legal Entities and Regulatory Compliance[1]

A1.1 INTRODUCTION

Most countries have introduced laws for the criminal liability of legal entities. The criminal liability of legal entities has been spreading since the end of the last century as a result of the process of international harmonization in the European Union (1997–2000).

The main reasons for the introduction of a criminal liability system of legal entities in the legal system are, in general terms, the perception of companies as a focus of commission of crimes, and the need to involve the partners and the companies.

A1.2 TYPIFIED CONDUCTS

Legal entities are criminally liable for crimes committed in their name or by them, and in their direct or indirect benefit, by their legal representatives or by those who are authorized to make decisions on behalf of the legal entity or who hold faculties of organization and control within it.

They are also criminally liable for crimes committed in the exercise of social activities and on behalf of and for their direct or indirect benefit, by those who, being subject to the authority of the natural persons mentioned in the previous paragraph, have been able to carry out the acts for having seriously failed to comply with those duties of supervision, monitoring, and control of its activity, taking into account the specific circumstances of the case.

---

[1]Written by Jordi Lapiedra Cros, lawyer and partner of BiG Advocats SLP, specializing in European and Spanish regulation.

Legal entities can be exempt from liability if the crime is committed by people indicated in the first case, and the following conditions are met:

- The administrative body has adopted and effectively executed, before committing the offense, organizational and management models that include the appropriate surveillance and control measures to prevent crimes of the same nature or to significantly reduce the risk of its commission.
- The supervision of the functioning and compliance of the implemented prevention model has been entrusted to an organ of the legal entity with autonomous powers of initiative and control or that has been legally entrusted with the task of supervising the effectiveness of the internal controls of the legal entity.
- The author or individual authors have committed the crime by fraudulently evading the organization and prevention models.
- There has been no omission or insufficient practice of its supervisory, monitoring, and control functions by the organ of the legal entity with autonomous powers of initiative and control or legally entrusted with the task of supervising the effectiveness of internal controls of the legal entity.

The cases in which the previous circumstances can only be subject to partial certification, this circumstance will be assessed for the purpose of mitigating the penalty.

A1.3   CRIMES ATTRIBUTABLE TO LEGAL ENTITIES

The liability of legal entities is limited to several crimes of the Criminal Code, among which we highlight those related to accounting fraud:

- Scams
- Punishable insolvencies
- Money laundering
- Against the public treasury and against Social Security

A1.4   ORGANIZATION AND MANAGEMENT MODELS

The organization and management models of legal entities that include appropriate surveillance and control measures to prevent crimes, or to significantly reduce the risk of their occurrence, are exemptions from liability if they meet the following requirements:

- Identify the activities where the crimes that should be prevented can be committed.
- They establish the protocols or procedures that specify the process of formation of the will of the legal entity, of decision-making, and their execution in relation to them.
- They have management models with adequate financial resources to prevent the commission of the crimes that must be prevented.
- Impose the obligation to report possible risks and noncompliance to the body in charge of monitoring the operation and compliance of the prevention model.
- Establish a disciplinary system that adequately sanctions noncompliance with the measures established by the model.
- They perform a periodic verification of the model and its eventual modification when relevant infractions of its dispositions are revealed, or when there are changes in the organization, in the control structure or in the developed activity that make them necessary.

A1.5   MODELS OF PREVENTION AND CONTROL

The models of prevention and control have a description of the key elements of the legal entity, human, organizational, and documentary, and are applied to prevent the legal entity and its personnel from infringing the law and, in particular, performing acts that may be classified as a crime.

The main goal of the prevention and control model is for all levels of the company to be involved and ensure the real and effective application of the prevention and control measures prescribed in the model, so that through self-regulation the elimination of risk behaviors is achieved.

The basic structure of a prevention and control model could be the following.

- Elaboration of a risk map. The prevention and control model must identify the activities in which the crimes that should be prevented can be committed.
- Adoption of an ethical code. A document that describes the key elements of the legal entity—human, organizational, and documentary—and establishes behavioral patterns to be followed so there are no infringements of the law.

- Decision-making protocol. Regulation of the process of formation of the will of the legal entity, of decision-making and their execution.
- Regulatory structure. Elaboration of a set of standards and management models suitable to prevent the commission of crimes that must be prevented during the activity of the company.
- Control structure. Agency in charge of monitoring the operation and compliance of the prevention model.
- Ethical channel. It allows informing of risks and noncompliance to the agency in charge of control.
- Disciplinary regime. Legislation that adequately sanctions noncompliance of the measures established by the model.
- Training and awareness program. It guarantees due knowledge of the prevention and control model by the entire structure of the company.
- Periodic verification. The model of prevention and control must be permanently updated when changes in the organization or the applicable regulation occur, and must also be reviewed in the case of relevant infractions.

REFERENCES

AENOR. (2015). *Sistemas de gestión de compliance.* Directrices. UNE-ISO 19600:2015.

Fiscaleneral del Estado. (2016). *Circular 1/2016 sobre la responsabilidad penal de las personas jurídicas conforme a la reforma del Código Penal efectuada por Ley Orgánica 1/2015.*

Organic Law 5/2010, June 22, through which the Penal Code was modified.

Organic Law 1/2015, March 30, through which the Organic Law 10/1995 is modified, November 23 of the Penal Code.

Porres Ortiz de Urbina, E. (2016). Responsabilidad penal de las personas jurídicas. *El Derecho.* (February 15).

Roig Altozano, M. (2012). La responsabilidad penal de las personas jurcas: Societas delinquere et puniri potest, *Noticias Jurcas* (February 1). http://noticias .juridicas.com/conocimiento/articulos-doctrinales/4746-la-responsabilidad-penal-de-las-personas-juridicas:-societas-delinquere-et-puniri-potest/.

Audit Program for the Identification of Fraud Risks

This work program has been elaborated from:

REA-REGA (2015): Technical teacher for the practical application of the ISA 240, Register of Economists Auditors REA-REGA, November.
ICJCE (2015): Planning tools: "ISA-ES 240," *Instituto de Censores Jurados de Cuentas de España* (Institute of Chartered Accountants of Spain), April.

A2.1   OBJECTIVE

The objective is planning the identification of risks in the scope of the auditor's responsibilities regarding fraud in the audit of annual accounts, in the sense of obtaining reasonable certainty that the annual accounts considered as a whole are free of material inaccuracies due to fraud (intentional error) or error.

   In this sense, the auditor's goals are to:

- Identify and assess the risks of material error in the annual accounts due to fraud.
  - Obtain sufficient and adequate evidence of audit regarding the assessed risks of material error due to fraud, by designing and implementing appropriate responses.
- Respond adequately to the fraud or to the signs of fraud identified during the performance of the audit.

PROCEDURE OF IDENTIFICATION AND ASSESSMENT OF FRAUD RISK			
	Year X Following	Year X Planning	Year X-1
A) IN RELATION WITH CONDUCTS AND FACTS			
	Y/N/NP	Y/N/NP	Y/N/NP
1. Are there precedents or suspicions that the entity has ever had any of the following circumstances?			
—Manipulation, falsification, or alteration of accounting records or of the supporting documentation from which the annual accounts are prepared.			
—Distortion or intentional omission of facts, transactions or other significant information in the annual accounts.			
—Intentional misapplication of accounting principles relating to amounts, classification, the form of presentation or disclosure of information.			
2. Have unusual or unexpected relationships been detected between the auditor and the management?			
3. Have accounting estimate situations been identified that could cause biases (overvaluation or undervaluation)?			
4. Have unusual or unexpected significant transactions been identified?			
5. Has any error been identified, whether material or not, that could be the result of fraud, in which management is involved?			

	Y/N/NP	Y/N/NP	Y/N/NP
6. By the knowledge of the company, is it known or suspected that there may be an incentive or an element of pressure to the company's management, from internal or external organizations, for management to provide fraudulent financial information, in order to achieve an expected (and perhaps unrealistic) objective of profits or financial results?			
7. Do you have the feeling that a person from the management or an employee could avoid the internal control?			
8. Is there a culture or environment that favors or provides the opportunity to perpetrate the commission of fraud?			
9. Is there any perception of unusual or unexplained changes in the behavior or the lifestyle of members of the management or employees, which could be indicative of fraudulent behavior?			
10. Have you noticed the existence of any of the following situations that can cause tension to commit fraud?			
—The need to satisfy the expectations of third parties to obtain additional equity.			
—The granting of significant bonuses if unrealistic profit objectives are achieved.			
11. Is there a control environment that isn't effective, which can be an incentive to commit fraud?			

	Y/N/NP	Y/N/NP	Y/N/NP
12. Is there only one person who exercises the management? This can lead to a possible deficiency in internal control, since it offers the management the possibility of avoiding controls and being in a position to commit fraud			

Are risk factors identified?

YES	NO

Describe and transfer to the risk matrix.

	LOW	MEDIUM	HIGH
1.			
2.			
3.			
4.			

B) RISK FACTORS RELATED WITH FINANCIAL INFORMATION (ISA-ES 240 Annex 1)			
	Y/N/NP	Y/N/NP	Y/N/NP
1. High degree of competition and decline in margins?			
2. Operating losses with imminent threat of bankruptcy, enforcement or hostile takeover?			
3. New accounting, legal, or regulatory requirements?			
4. Management subjected to excessive pressure to meet third parties' requirements or expectations?			

	Y/N/NP	Y/N/NP	Y/N/NP
5. Need to obtain additional financing through external resources?			
6. Is there a limited capacity to meet financial requirements?			
7. Is the personal financial situation of management members threatened by the financial evolution of the company?			
8. The rewards to management and senior positions depend on the achievement of certain objectives?			
9. Are there significant transactions with related parties, alien to the normal course of business, with related entities unaudited or audited by another auditor?			
10. Are there are assets, liabilities, income, or expenses based on significant estimates that imply subjective judgments or uncertainties difficult to corroborate?			
11. Are there are significant, unusual or highly complex transactions, especially in dates near the closing date of the year?			
12. Significant cross-border operations or transactions carried out abroad?			
13. Bank accounts or operations in tax havens?			
14. Difficulty to determine the entities or people with participation in the control of the entity?			
15. High turnover of members of top management, legal advisors, auditors?			

	Y/N/NP	Y/N/NP	Y/N/NP
16. Ineffective selection of accounting, internal audit, or information technology employees?			
17. Known history of breach of regulations? Existing lawsuits?			
18. Excessive interest of the Management in maintaining or increasing the entity's profits?			
19. The entity does not correct the known deficiencies in the internal control?			
20. Interest of management to unduly minimize the profits for fiscal reasons?			
21. Does the owner–manager distinguish between personal and business transactions?			
22. Are there recurrent attempts by management to justify a parallel or inadequate accounting based on its relative importance?			

Are risk factors identified?

YES	NO

Describe and transfer to the risk matrix.

	LOW	MEDIUM	HIGH
1.			
2.			
3.			
4.			

C) IN RELATION TO POSSIBLE EMBEZZLEMENT OF ASSETS (NIA-ES 240 Annex 1)			
	Y/N/NP	Y/N/NP	Y/N/NP
1. Misappropriation of income from accounts receivable?			
2. Diversion of funds from company bank accounts to personal accounts?			
3. Subtraction of physical assets or intellectual property?			
4. Subtraction of inventory for personal use or for sale?			
5. Subtraction of waste material for resale?			
6. Disclosure of data to the competition in exchange for payment?			
7. Payment to fictitious suppliers in exchange of services that haven't been provided?			
8. Payment to fictitious employees?			
9. Use of company assets for personal use?			
10. Fake records or documents, in order to hide that the assets disappeared without authorization?			
11. Are there a lot of insurance claims for asset losses?			
12. Bad relationships between the company and workers with personal situations that produce financial stress?			
13. Known or foreseeable future layoff of employees?			
14. Promotions, compensation, or other rewards inconsistent with expectations?			

	Y/N/NP	Y/N/NP	Y/N/NP
15. Cash maintenance or handling of large amounts of cash?			
16. Small size, high value, and highly demanded inventory?			
17. Assets easily convertible to cash?			
18. Inadequate internal control over the assets?			
19. Inadequate supervision of top management expenses, travels, meals, or other reimbursement?			
20. Absence of documentation on transactions?			
21. Inadequate authorization and approval system for transactions?			
22. Lack of attention to the need for monitoring or reducing the risks related to the misappropriation of assets?			
23. Tolerance to minor subtractions?			

Are risk factors identified?

YES	NO

Describe and transfer to the risk matrix.

	LOW	MEDIUM	HIGH
1.			
2.			
3.			
4.			

D) RISK FACTORS RELATED TO SALES			
	Y/N/NP	Y/N/NP	Y/N/NP
1. Does the company register significant sales before proceeding to the delivery of the products or services?			
2. Is there a high volume of returns after the close of the year that exceeds the usual?			
3. Are there sales operations or transactions that are unusual, complex, abnormal or significant?			
4. Are there substantial sales at the end of the accounting period? Does this make sense compared to previous trimesters, or compared to the close of the year on previous years?			
5. Have revenues been accounted for in the period in which they accrue?			

Describe the types of income and the income-generating transactions that exist in the audited company, as well as the possibility that it may lead to a risk of fraud.

Are risk factors identified?

YES	NO

Describe and transfer to the risk matrix.

	LOW	MEDIUM	HIGH
1.			
2.			
3.			
4.			

E) IN RELATION TO ESTIMATES (ISA 540)			
	Y/N/NP	Y/N/NP	Y/N/NP
1. Impairment of the value of credits for irregular business operations?			
2. Unusual obsolesce of inventory?			
3. Changes in depreciation methods or assets life cycles?			
4. (Irregular) Provision relating to the book value of an investment when there is uncertainty about its recoverability?			
5. Irregular posting of the costs derived from the resolution of lawsuits and sentences?			
6. Dubious posting of complex financial instruments, which aren't negotiated in active and open markets.			
7. Are there assets or liabilities acquired in a business combination, including goodwill?			
8. Are there transactions that imply exchange of assets or liabilities between independent parties without monetary compensation?			

Are risk factors identified?

YES	NO

Describe and transfer to the risk matrix.

	LOW	MEDIUM	HIGH
1.			
2.			
3.			
4.			

F) DISCREPANCIES IN THE ACCOUNTING RECORDS (ISA-ES 240 Annex 3)			
	Y/N/NP	Y/N/NP	Y/N/NP
1. Transactions that have not been registered in full or in a timely manner, amount, price, accounting period, classification, policy of the company?			
2. Balances or transactions without documentary justification or authorization?			
3. Last minute adjustments that significantly affect the results?			
4. Evidence of employee access to systems and inconsistent records with the access they need to perform their authorized task?			
5. Confidences or complaints to the auditor regarding alleged fraud?			

Are risk factors identified?

YES	NO

Describe and transfer to the risk matrix.

	LOW	MEDIUM	HIGH
1.			
2.			
3.			
4.			

G) CONTRADICTORY EVIDENCE OR LACK OF EVIDENCE THAT INCLUDES (ISA-ES 240 Annex 3)			
	Y/N/NP	Y/N/NP	Y/N/NP
1. Absence of documentation?			
2. Documents that seem to have been altered?			
3. Unexplained significant reconciliation items?			
4. Unusual discrepancies between the company's records and the confirmation answers?			
5. A high number of installments and other adjustments made in the records of accounts receivable?			
6. Availability only of photocopies and electronic documents in cases where the existence of original documents is expected?			
7. Unusual changes in the balance sheet, or changes in trends or ratios or important relationships in the financial statements. For example, faster growth of accounts receivable than revenue?			
8. Inconsistent, vague, or unlikely answers from management, or from the employees in the investigations, or the analytical procedures performed?			

Are risk factors identified?

YES	NO

Describe and transfer to the risks matrix.

	LOW	MEDIUM	HIGH
1.			
2.			
3.			
4.			

H) RELATIONSHIP WITH MANAGEMENT AND ITS RELATIONSHIP WITH THE PREVIOUS AUDITOR			
	Y/N/NP	Y/N/NP	Y/N/NP
1. Are there frequent disputes of management with the current auditor or its predecessor?			
2. Are there unreasonable demands made by management to the auditor, such as unrealistic time restrictions for the completion of the audit?			
3. Imposition of restrictions on the auditor that inappropriately limit access to people or information?			
4. Overbearing attitude of management in its dealings with the auditor, especially if this entails attempts to influence the scope of the auditor's work?			
5. Irrational requests to change members in the audit team?			
6. Provision of information with unusual delays, incomplete, or misleading?			
7. Lack of willingness to adopt corrective measures regarding the identified audit differences or internal control weaknesses?			

Are risk factors identified?

YES	NO

Describe and transfer to the risk matrix.

	LOW	MEDIUM	HIGH
1.			
2.			
3.			
4.			

A2.2 CONCLUSION

The fraud risks identified should be treated as significant and, as such, knowledge of the company's controls for said risks and of the audit responses that must be established for each of the risks should be obtained.

ANSWERS TO RISKS ASSESSED FOR INCORRECTNESS DUE TO FRAUD

Global Answers

Professional skepticism is accentuated in performing the audit when we have evidence of fraud. For example:

- Through a greater sensibility in selecting the nature and extend of the documentation to be examined, as support for transactions considered material.
- Through greater knowledge of the need to corroborate the explanations or statements of the management body on matters considered material.
- The auditor will evaluate whether by the identification of these audit risks, the quality control review of the order is required.

In determining these responses:

	WORKSHEET
Conscientious assignment of the work team	
Evaluation of accounting policies, especially Management's estimates and complex transactions	
Introduction of unpredictability elements in the selection of the nature, timing and extension of evidence	

Answers Based on the Valuation Obtained from the Fraud Risks and According to the Professional Opinion of the Auditor

	WORKSHEET
Go to inventories without prior notice.	
Substantive or control tests or a combination of both.	
Physical inspection.	
Confirm with customers in addition to balances, contracts, commercial discounts	
Tests on intermediate dates.	
Increase the sample size.	
We will place special emphasis on the estimates, analysis and calculation method	
We will place special emphasis on significant or unusual transactions, especially if they are produced at the closing of exercise or with related parties.	

(Continued)

EVALUATION OF THE AUDIT EVIDENCE

	WORKSHEET
Analytical procedures at the closure of the audit are indicative of possible material impropriety due to a previously unidentified fraud.	
If in the work done, the auditor considers that a document analyzed may not be authentic, he will start detailed investigations of the matter.	
If there are identified inaccuracies, evaluate if they are indicative of fraud and their implications in the audit report.	
Reconsider the assessment of fraud risk and its involvement in the audit in the case of inaccuracies in which there are reasons to believe that they are or may be the result of a fraud in which management is involved.	
If it is confirmed that the annual accounts contain material inaccuracies due to fraud, or conclusions can't be reached, evaluate the implications this fact will have in our audit report.	

Impossibility of the Auditor to Continue with the Charge—if Applicable

If, from the conclusions obtained from this document, and as a consequence of one or several material inaccuracies due to fraud or indication of fraud, we question our ability to continue doing the audit we must:

- Determine professional and legal responsibilities. The auditor will evaluate the need to consult a legal advisor, other auditors or the corporation.
- Consider whether to give up the assignment. We must consider what is established in the Audit Law and discuss and inform the management and the responsible for the company's governance of the resignation.
- Inform the authorities (ICAC and Mercantile Registry).

Obtain Letter of Manifestations

Obtain from the management and, when applicable, from the responsible for the company's governance, written statements on what is established in the requirement 39 of the ISA-ES 240.

Communications to the Management and to the Company's Governing Body

If we identify a fraud or we obtain information that indicates the possible existence of fraud, we will communicate and document it (orally or written), through the partner responsible for the charge, in the appropriated management level, and to the company's governing body, which is mainly responsible for the prevention and detection of fraud, as well as the issues relevant to their responsibilities.

Communication to the Regulatory and Supervision Authorities

If a fraud is identified, we will determine our responsibility to inform it to a third party outside the company, documenting such communication when appropriate. We will seek legal advice if necessary.

Conclusion

(A) In accordance with the program and detailed worksheets, we consider that we have not identified material inaccuracies in the audited financial statements due to fraud.

(B) We identified material inaccuracies due to fraud in the financial statements, whose valuation, if possible its quantification, is reflected in the worksheets indicated above, and we have communicated it:

a) To the management and to the responsible of the audited company's governance.	YES	NO
b) To the regulatory and supervisor authorities, as established in the audit regulations.	YES	NO

(Continued)

In Consequence

c) We have assessed our professional responsibilities.	YES	NO
d) We offer our resignation as auditors of the company, and if applicable, we communicated it to the Supervisory Body.	YES	NO

List of Companies Mentioned in the Book and Section in which They Appear

Adelphi Pharmaceuticals	4.2
Afinsa	10.1
AM Best	3.3
Amazon	6.3
Anicom, Inc.	9.3
Apple	6.3
Arthur Andersen	3.2
Banesto	8.5
Bank of America	8.5
Bar Chris Construction Corporation	2.3
Bausch & Lomb	9.1
BNP Paribas	3.3
Bompreço	4.2
City of Glasgow Bank	3.2
Citigroup	2.4
Clasificadora de Riesgo Humphreys	3.3
Coca-Cola	1.2
Colonial Bank	6.2
Companhia Portuguesa de Rating	3.3
Compañía Holandesa de las Indias Orientales	2.2
Credit Suisse	2.4
Del Global Technologies	9.3
Deloitte Touche	4.2
Dental International	8.3
Dental Finance	8.3
Deutsche Bank	11.2
Disco	4.2
Dominion Bond Rating Service	3.3
Durex	6.2